PENGUIN BOOKS

Cosmopolitan Guide to Student Life

Louise Clarke studied History of Art at University College London, where she first became involved in student journalism. She became a member of the first *Cosmopolitan* Student Advisory Board, published her features in the *Daily Telegraph* and the *Sunday Correspondent*, and took a part-time job writing listings for the *Guardian*. After graduation she became editor of the University of London newspaper, *London Student*, Britain's largest student newspaper, for which she won the *Guardian*/NUS Student Media Award. Since 1992 she has been Press and PR Officer at the National Union of Students and probably knows more about students than any other person in the country! Louise has continued her freelance career, particularly contributing to the *Independent*, the *Guardian*, *Cosmopolitan* and *Marie Claire*. She has also edited the *Time Out Student Guide 1995*.

COSMOPOLITAN
Guide to **Student Life**

LOUISE CLARKE

PENGUIN BOOKS

PENGUIN BOOKS

Published by the Penguin Group
Penguin Books Ltd, 27 Wrights Lane, London W8 5TZ, England
Penguin Books USA Inc., 375 Hudson Street, New York, New York 10014, USA
Penguin Books Australia Ltd, Ringwood, Victoria, Australia
Penguin Books Canada Ltd, 10 Alcorn Avenue, Toronto, Ontario, Canada M4V 3B2
Penguin Books (NZ) Ltd, 182–190 Wairau Road, Auckland 10, New Zealand

Penguin Books Ltd, Registered Offices: Harmondsworth, Middlesex, England

First published 1996
10 9 8 7 6 5 4 3 2 1

Copyright © The National Magazine Company, 1996
All rights reserved

The moral right of the author has been asserted

The expression *Cosmopolitan* is the trade mark of The National Magazine
Company Limited and The Hearst Corporation, registered in the UK and the
USA, and other principal countries of the world, and is the absolute property of
The National Magazine Company Limited and The Hearst Corporation. The
use of this trade mark other than with the express permission of The National
Magazine Company or The Hearst Corporation is strictly prohibited.

Set in 10.5/13 pt Monotype Baskerville
Typeset by Datix International Limited, Bungay, Suffolk
Printed in England by Clays Ltd, St Ives plc

Except in the United States of America, this book is sold subject
to the condition that it shall not, by way of trade or otherwise, be lent,
re-sold, hired out, or otherwise circulated without the publisher's
prior consent in any form of binding or cover other than that in
which it is published and without a similar condition including this
condition being imposed on the subsequent purchaser

Contents

Chapter 1 / **Before You Go, Freshers Week and Beyond** 1

Chapter 2 / **Money** 15

Chapter 3 / **Study** 50

Chapter 4 / **Living** 65

Chapter 5 / **Health and Happiness** 93

Chapter 6 / **Sex and Relationships** 119

Chapter 7 / **Making Your Mark and Making the Most of Your College Life** 130

Chapter 8 / **Travel and Making the Most of Vacations** 142

Chapter 9 / **Getting Ahead – Graduation and Beyond** 148

Chapter 10 / **How to Handle the Job Hunt** 157

Chapter 11 / **Further Information** 174

Chapter 1 / Before You Go, Freshers Week and Beyond

Going to college has to be one of the most knee-trembling and stomach-turning times in anyone's life. Clutching your acceptance letter, there's a sudden realization that, after months of exams, interviews, worry and wonder, this is it. The thought of leaving friends, boyfriends, girlfriends, parents, pets and the four walls of your bedroom for the big, wide world of student life cannot fail to induce a mixture of anxiety and excitement. A whirlwind of questions races through your head and panic begins to set in. What will happen? How will you meet people? Where are you going to live? None of these questions can be answered. Not before you've spent three years studying will you really know what was in store for you. But one thing is certain: everyone else is feeling the same. You and every other first-year student – freshers as you will be known – are about to embark on a huge adventure, and to worry is totally forgivable.

But right now, as well as an awful lot of the 'what if?' and 'what will happen?' kind of questions, you have quite a few practical problems to deal with. For a start, you've got to condense your life's collection of tat and rubbish into a select few items to cram into the boot of your parents' car or into a selection of bags you can carry yourself on a trip across country. You have to work out what you will need in unknown territory, and even Indiana Jones would be fazed by the possibilities. You've got to sort out money, get a bank account, work out a budget, get some money. You've got to find somewhere to live and to fit in. You've got to start thinking about the practicalities of studying. You've got to say goodbye. You've got to work out what to wear.

Many of your anxieties about what will happen and what you will do will be addressed within the first few days of arriving. Colleges, coping with thousands of freshers in the same state, year on year, have developed Freshers Weeks, and a hectic agenda of social events, meetings and making friends will leave you out of breath. The practical problems of sorting out your new life before you leave for college are up to you, however, and now is the time to get organized, to plot and plan.

What to Take with You

Let's face it. You have very little idea of what you are going to need. This is no school trip, this is going off to college, and you know you'll need a bit more than a lightweight waterproof coat and a selection of sandwiches. Nor is it a two-week package tour to Ibiza. Unless you plan to make frequent trips home, you will need to pack for the change in weather and for all occasions, not just the first fortnight of fresher engagements. You will need not only food, medicine, comfortable walking shoes, a jar of coffee and your teddy bear, but a good deal else besides. If you're going to go into a hall of residence it's best to give them a call and check on what's provided in the way of bedding and kitchen utensils before emptying your mum's linen cupboard and cutlery drawer into your rucksack. Draw up a list and work out what you have and what you will need. Now is the time to accept any gifts or hand-me-downs, and to pressure your parents into buying you a new duvet cover so that you can leave the Paddington Bear cover at home.

Check List

This isn't a definitive list, and is certainly more than one mere mortal can carry by public transport, but it's everything you'll wish you had at some point in the first term, so try to cadge a lift with family or friends and overload their car with as much as you have.

- duvet
- sheets
- pillow
- 2 towels
- large floor cushion or beanbag
- kettle
- jar of coffee, tea bags
- 2 plates
- 2 sets of knives, forks and spoons
- tin-opener
- 4 mugs
- 4 glass tumblers
- 2 breakfast bowls
- supply of food: cereal, long-life milk, tins of soup and beans bottle of wine
- posters, postcards and photos
- Blu-Tack
- swimming costume
- sports kit
- ball gown or party dress (you'll need it at least once in the first term)
- party shoes (unless you wear boots with your ball gown)
- lots of jumpers (student houses, libraries and lecture theatres are always cold)
- warm coat
- pyjamas (to wear outside when the fire alarm goes off in the middle of the night)
- Teddy
- A4 paper, pens and folders (although these can be bought cheaply from the student shop)
- diary
- address book
- dictionary (and just a few textbooks which might be useful – don't take your entire A-level course work and accompanying library of revision notes with you)

- light reading for relaxation
- stereo, tapes and CDs
- portable TV
- camera
- alarm clock
- aspirin, plasters, antiseptic cream
- vitamin supplements
- tampons
- huge bottle of shampoo
- shower gel (you don't want soap if you're going to share a bathroom)
- toothbrush and a huge supply of toothpaste
- make-up
- iron
- extension lead and multi-plug socket
- washing powder
- small sewing kit and a pair of scissors
- Phonecards
- pack of playing cards
- passport photos

Tips

Beg, borrow or steal whatever you can.

Accept all offers of going-away gifts of electrical appliances and a new pair of boots.

Consider carefully the limitations of your wardrobe. No one wants to look like a fashion victim on their first day and student style is fundamentally poverty-stricken grunge. Should you own an Armani suit leave it on its hanger at home. The only dressing up you'll be doing will be for the Freshers Ball and Christmas parties so plan accordingly for a lifetime of cardigans, leggings and Sloppy Joe jumpers.

Take as much food as you can before you parents notice the

diminishing supply in their own larder, but don't take too many perishables unless you're happy for them to be stolen from the communal fridge within minutes.

Saying Goodbye

Leaving is never easy. Despite your anxieties and fears about the huge changes about to happen, now is a time for hope and anticipation. If you're going to go off and make the most of these opportunities, you're going to have to leave things behind, even if it's just for a while. You will miss your friends like crazy, but you will make new friends and you won't lose your love for your old mates along the way. Your friends may be staying put, and they may be envious of your imminent independence and bid for breakaway freedom in a new town or city. They may be going off to different universities. Make sure you have one big night out before you go. It's an important ritual marking a big change in your life and theirs, but one which you should celebrate and which should cement your relationships. Take lots of snapshots so you can take happy memories with you. Remember the good times but don't fret that these will be the last.

It's going to be hard, but you have to make sure you give college life a good crack, so don't plan to come back home too soon or you may miss out on the crucial weeks of bonding with your course mates and new college friends at the start of term. Arrange to come back for the weekend four or five weeks after you've left, and stick to it. Homesickness is inevitable but if you have a date to look forward to, you'll find it much easier to cope with. Promise to write to them and make sure you get promises back to keep in touch. It's only ten weeks to Christmas vacation, anyway, and you can be sure of a good party when you all get together again then.

Leaving your parents and family will probably be much harder for them than it will be for you. They've cooked for you, cared for you, rowed with you and looked after you for so many years and now you're going off – it's your first real taste of independence – and your room will be empty. Many mums and dads get quite down when their offspring leave for university. True, their phone bills will be smaller and there will be less door slamming and waiting up all night for you to come home, but they'll miss you like mad and worry just the same. Make sure you call them regularly and if you come home for that big night out with your friends ensure you spend quality time with your parents as well. You can't just dump your washing and raid the fridge. They will worry about you, they'll be very proud of you, but they need you to show that you still need them and miss them.

If you're leaving a partner it's going to be even more heart-wrenching. It is easy to promise to be faithful and to try and keep a relationship going, and it's easy for them to promise the same. Go to college with an open mind, not a heavy heart. Things are going to change for you quite quickly, and few relationships from home make it through three years of student life, especially where distance is involved. It will be difficult to be realistic, but you have to realize your opportunities and you will have to throw yourself into student life without spending too many hours pining away, sobbing into your pillow with their photo by your side or queuing by the phone box for your nightly call to say 'I love you'. Of course, the fact that you're going off to university doesn't mean you must automatically finish your relationship. Who knows, this may be one of the tiny percentage of relationships which make it through to the end, but you can't let your passion stand in the way of your opportunity to make something of your life now. Promise to write to them, say once a week, but be firm with yourself and with them that you're only going to be able to make a go of college, and of the relationship, if you put things into perspective now. You're going to be pretty busy, spending a great deal of time studying and a fair amount of time making new mates (platonic mates, of course) and they need to understand that time will be at a premium. No one can afford to let their relationship become the priority: student life is too intensive to allow that level of distraction, so you must become practical about the amount of time you can spend on the relationship. Work out a solution, by keeping in touch with letters and the occasional phone call, and by sorting out a date to meet in a few weeks' time, once you've settled in and got your feet back on the ground.

Finding Somewhere to Live and Sorting out Money

Most freshers go into a hall of residence and there's more on this in the chapter on Living. If you haven't sorted out accommodation, call the accommodation office at your college. Every college has one and they will be able to sort you out, either with a last-minute hall room or with a list of reputable landlords in the area for a room in a shared student house or a bedsit. With all accommodation, you'll have to pay a deposit up front, which could be tricky given that you won't get your grant cheque until the first day of college. If you can't borrow from family or friends, now is the time to visit the bank.

All the banks and some of the building societies offer interest-free overdrafts to students, even as much as £1,000. Ideally you should shop around to find the best deal, but they all offer much the same. Things have changed quite a lot recently in the world of student banking and it's quite easy to change branches and even banks. If you need money in advance, for your accommodation deposit, for example, take along to any bank on the High Street some form of identification and the letter from your local education authority confirming that your tuition fees will be paid. If you like the sound of their student deals and can be assured that there's a branch of the bank on your campus you can go right ahead and open your account and organize an overdraft there and then. Once you get to college you may find it easier to transfer the account to the campus branch, but there's nothing to stop you opening the account at home and arranging all your bank details now. Then, once you arrive, you'll have somewhere to pay in your grant cheque and have all the freebies and overdraft you may need. If you decide you'd prefer to bank with another bank or building society, you can close down the first account and move your money and overdraft elsewhere with comparative ease.

Last-minute Worries

Having packed your parents' car boot to the brim, arranged your accommodation, opened a bank account, sobbed on your friends' shoulders and shared a long, lingering last kiss with your loved one, you are ready for the off. Before you pull away from the kerb, check you have everything you'll need for registering at college. You will need your actual birth certificate (not a photocopy) and your exam certificates (but don't worry too much if you're still waiting for A-level certificates to come through as you can show these at a later date). You'll also need your medical card to sign on at a doctor's surgery or a medical centre on campus. Take along any correspondence you've had to date from your department or from the university, and take letters from the local education authority about your grant. Make sure you have their phone number and address. Grant cheques are often delayed and you may need to call them to chase it up, so you'll need their details and any reference number assigned to you. Make sure everyone at home has your address and contact numbers in case of emergency. Finally, double check on the tin-opener and your teddy bear, and then you can set off into the distance. This is it. Now you're really going.

Arriving

The scene's the same at every campus in the country: thousands of nervous, but excited, freshers unloading boxes and beanbags from Volvos and old vans, mothers dabbing at their eyes with tissues and dads looking proud but stern. Don't be embarrassed by the presence or absence of your parents. No one's noticing them. In fact no one's noticing anyone. It is an overwhelming experience for virtually everyone. If you're going into halls, you will arrive and report to the main reception to pick up your key and hand over any deposit cheque. Then it's a trundle down the corridor to unlock the door of your new home for the next three terms. Expect a bare-walled room with dodgy seventies curtains, rough brown carpet and a simple single bed, plus a desk (with three standard shelves), a small chest of drawers and a wardrobe so small it's an insult to your clothes. Once the boxes and beanbags have been unloaded and parents have tearfully departed, it's just you, the unpacking and the bare walls. Get on with the decoration at break-neck speed – the longer the walls are bare, the more instant and more intense the depression will be. You can be amazed at the difference a few posters and some snaps of your pet dog can make to a room. Unpack your books, your crockery, make the bed and fix up the stereo, and prepare for the fun to begin.

If you haven't had a knock on the door within the first few hours it'll be up to you to make the first call on your neighbour. Don't be nervous – this is a crucial ritual in student life and a moment you will look back and laugh at almost as soon as an hour later. Whoever you find will be so pleased to share a conversation and unburden their own nervousness and excitement that you can be sure of an interesting night. Crack open the wine or whip up a cup of instant coffee and get nattering. It may sound daunting but you'll find it almost natural. If there's a communal kitchen, take your wine or coffee in and before long you'll find you have a party going on. The people that you meet on the first night away may not be the people you spend the rest of your college days with but it will be an interesting time. Don't panic if you can't stand them – you won't be in a position to make such judgements, anyway, being so overwhelmed with anxiety and hungry for shared experiences. Having met a few people, suggest a tour of the campus, or the town, to get your bearings and call in on the student union bar or local pub to check out the possibilities for your new social life.

Your First Day

Try not to wake on your first day with a hangover. This is going to be one of the most bewildering, confusing and dull days of your whole college career. Endless queuing, endless questioning, and inevitable boredom are the ingredients of everyone's first day, alleviated only by the people that you meet in queues and corridors who will eventually become some of your best friends in all the world. You should have had information through from the university as to where you should report on the first day. Clutching your certificates, letters of acceptance, a map of the campus and your new-found friends from the night before, set off for registration. Some universities arrange a photographer to take everyone's photographs, otherwise a couple of rolls of passport photos are going to be very useful. You need to arrange your college identity card and register before you can pick up your grant cheque and your National Union of Students (NUS) card from the student union. Then you can report to your department to sign up for course options and find out details about your timetable.

Teaching for freshers doesn't usually begin until about a week after registration but think again if this sounds like a week off. It isn't. It's a hectic week of form-filling, knocking on doors and attending meetings. You will get to meet your tutor, students from the years above and other freshers starting your course. Many departments hold reception parties where you can chat informally to the tutors over a glass of cheap red wine and some cheese nibbles. You will be given a copy of a reading list – a huge list of recommended course books. Under no circumstances should you rush to the book shop to spend your entire grant on these books. Only some of them will be relevant and this will be apparent only after you've chosen your course options, and each course option tutor will supply you with a further reading list. Most of the books should be available in the library, and, if not, check out the noticeboard in your department common room or office for ads from second- and third-years who want to sell their old books. Find out as much as you can about all the course options available and check how they can fit into your timetable. If there are obvious clashes, don't panic as it will probably be possible to take these options next term or even in later years. Most departments elect course representatives from among the students to represent student views in departmental meetings and on the college-wide Student Representative Council, which is usually part of the student union. This is a great opportunity to get really involved and make an impression, as well as a good way to meet people on other courses and in other departments.

Every student is assigned a personal tutor and you should get to meet them for a five-minute chat at some time in the first week. Your personal tutor is there to offer academic advice but also to offer advice on other matters. They can deal with most of your problems and point you in the direction of help if and when you need it. If, for some reason, you feel you don't like your personal tutor, you can easily change to another without offending anyone's feelings. Most tutors have special hours set aside when they are available in their office to meet their students and discuss how things are going.

Having sorted out your course, it's time to sort out your extra-curricular interests. You will usually collect your NUS card from the student union. This is a national student identity card and entitles you to discounts with many chain stores, local shops, theatres, cinemas, galleries and museums. Virtually every college in the country is affiliated to the National Union of Students, but those which aren't produce their own individual cards. The student union is the hub of student life. Everything happens here and you will find it the source of information, advice and entertainment. The student union provides welfare information, debt counselling and advice on problems with your course. Should you ever have cause for complaint this is the place to come to. They will also provide much of your social life. The student union will run hundreds of sports clubs, social clubs and societies, incorporating everything from parachuting and potholing to debating and drama. Within the first week there will be a huge freshers fair, where all the clubs and societies have stands, alongside many commercial companies, political groups and campaign groups who want to meet students. Here you can sign up for any number of clubs and societies – but don't go crazy. Pick and choose with at least some care. This isn't your last opportunity to get involved – just the first – and if you decide to take up Latin American dancing or korfball at a later date there will be no problem. It usually costs a small sum to join, around £3 according to the nature of the sport or society and the equipment involved. But you'll find everything's provided, from canoes and diving equipment to potters' wheels and chess sets. Whether your interest is in student media or aqua-aerobics you'll find something that catches your eye. Give it a go. You will need other interests apart from your books and the bar, and college clubs and societies are the best way to find new hobbies and discover new things about yourself.

Your student union will also provide all the evening entertainment you could dream of, and at a fraction of the price anywhere else. Bars are stocked with cheap beer and the best bands in the country regularly tour the student union circuit. Discos, quiz nights and karaoke are all part of the timetable of fun and a special effort is made during Freshers Week to ensure you have the most active social life. Many hold special Freshers Balls and Intro Party nights to get you into the swing and create a focus for your first weekend away. You should make every effort to go and to have a good time. Most put on big-name bands, comedians, food, drink and DJs. Check the dress code before you go, though. It may be a ball-gown affair, in which case don your glad rags; however, attending a leggings-and-Lycra type of do in pink taffeta could leave you feeling sadly out of place and uncomfortable all evening.

Take care not to drink too much and be wary of predatory second- and third-years who make a sport of seducing innocent first-years in the heady excitement of Freshers Week. But throw yourself into having a good time and meeting as many people as possible. You may find you make some 'friends' during Freshers Week that you will spend the rest of your college years trying to avoid. For this reason, try not to get too carried away or too intimate sexually with any of the people you meet in the first week. There will be lots of opportunities to chase up potential partners later on in the term, or even over the next three or four years, and there is no reason to rush into relationships in these first few days, however appealing it may seem.

With your course details arranged, your social life organized and a full timetable of academic and non-academic events lined up for the next few weeks, you have time to sort out practicalities. You will need to find out about the library and arrange an induction visit for a tour. Most college libraries run these in association with the departments or you can simply go along and ask for a quick guide of all the services. As well as course books, college libraries keep periodicals, newspapers and magazines. The computer search system will need some explaining but it is simple to pick up and will allow you to find relevant books and articles that might not be on your reading list. You will also need to visit the computer centre in your college and find out about its services, opening times and how to book yourself in. Most tutors expect students to hand in word-processed essays and projects now and the computer centre can provide training in computer programs as well as access to a number of terminals for you to type your work.

You will also want to pay a visit to the college medical centre or doctor's surgery and sign yourself on before you fall ill. It's quite likely that you will get ill at some time in the first term. Different towns harbour different germs and a hectic social life combined with an erratic diet (no more of Mum's food) means you may be more susceptible to colds, flu and tummy bugs. The medical centre will also provide cervical smear tests and offer advice on contraception; it's worth going along for a medical as soon as you can.

Going off to college is a drama, but it doesn't have to be a trauma. It is an exciting time, as well as bewildering and frightening. But the fact that there are hundreds and thousands of freshers going through the same thing up and down the country, and millions have gone through it already, should help you realize that it's not as bad as you might think. It is a new beginning of a new life and after the first few days it's almost plain sailing all the way. Until exam time, that is.

Chapter 2 / **Money**

Money is the one thing that unites all students in exasperation – there's never enough of it. Whatever trials and torments your tutors might put you through it's nothing compared with the hoops and hurdles you will have to jump in order to balance your books financially. Even then it is certainly possible to find yourself getting into debt and running into real problems. Whatever your incomings and outgoings might be, you will probably find it almost unbearable at some point through your student days. But stick with it. There are ways and means of surviving, and you won't be poor for ever.

Most students these days have come to terms with living with overdrafts, loans and letters from the bank manager. It is part of the ritual of student life and you can rest assured you won't be alone in the red. However, you have to make sure you have claimed everything you are entitled to and you should find out as much as possible about the various options for loans, overdrafts, the government's access funds and various hardship grants available.

Then it's up to you to try and keep your spending within the limits of your funds and to cut as many corners as possible. Some may have the luxury of parents and relatives with deep pockets and generous hearts, but many will not, and you may find you have to take on part-time jobs to earn your crust. Otherwise it will be a case of more begging and more borrowing to keep you on track to the end of your course.

But don't worry – it's not all bad news. Student loans are written off if you haven't repaid them after twenty-five years or by the age of fifty.

Basic Finance Facts: Where Will You Get Your Money From?

Grants

Many students are entitled to a grant towards the cost of their maintenance (rent, food and basic living expenses). The amount of grant is determined by the government, who set the sum each year. You have to apply to your local education authority, usually based in your county council office, which distributes the funds on behalf of the government.

Whether or not you are entitled to a grant depends on several factors. Firstly, the type of course you are planning to study; secondly, your parents', your own or your partner's income; and thirdly, whether or not you have received a grant previously.

There are various types of course which can entitle you to a grant. Your local education authority is obliged to pay a grant (a mandatory award) if your course is a designated 'advanced' course, which generally speaking means all full-time or sandwich courses for a first degree, HND or certificate of comparable status and for initial teaching training (including the Postgraduate Certificate of Education). For other courses, such as part-time postgraduate courses, A-level and Ordinary National Diploma and BTEC courses, the local education authority is not obliged to give you a grant, but can make a grant if it so desires (a discretionary award). Unfortunately fewer and fewer local education authorities have the resources to pay discretionary grants these days and demand is very high. If you plan to study a course which does not command a mandatory award you should try and find out as soon as possible if there may be a likelihood you will be refused a grant.

The rules concerning how much grant you will get change slightly each year but are largely based on either your parents' or your own income. If you are over twenty-five, or if you have no living parent, if you have been married for over two years or have been totally self-supporting for at least three years before the beginning of the academic year, then you will be classed as an 'independent' and your parents' income will not count.

For most students, their parents' income is the basis used to set the amount they will receive as a grant. It is then up to your parents to make up the difference, although they are not obliged to by law and some parents do refuse. If this happens, there's not a lot you can do, except plead with them or try to find the money from some other source. The government sets the levels when parents should begin contributing, and the rules are quite complicated. It is best to start researching how much you can get and how much your parents may have to pay as soon as you can. The Department of Education and Employment produces a booklet, *A Brief Guide to Grants and Loans*, with all the latest information on the levels set for the year. (Its address is in the Further Information chapter.)

Forms to apply for a grant are available from your local education authority and you will need your wits about you to fill them in. You should fill in the form when you start applying to colleges, and as soon as you have been accepted you must send off one of the forms (the college acceptance form) to your college, which will confirm to the local education authority that you have a place. Your parents will have to complete an assessment form and present proof of their earnings and the tax they have paid and details of their mortgage and other outgoings which can be deducted from their income to make the calculation.

Grant applications are a complicated business and local education authorities sometimes make mistakes so it helps if you can understand the rules and try and work out what you think you might be entitled to.

Your local education authority will also be responsible for paying your tuition fees but don't worry, as this is paid straight to the college, and there are only a few exceptions for students who are not eligible, for example students from overseas.

Your grant will be paid by cheque in three instalments to coincide with the start of each term. It is normally sent directly to the college and at the beginning of each term you will have to queue up at the college grant office to pick up the cheque on production of your student identity card. Sometimes grant cheques arrive late, usually because of bad administration on the part of the local education authority. If this happens, and your cheque has not arrived, you should contact your student union, who can telephone the local education authority on your behalf and chase up the cheque, and they may also be able to advance you an amount of money in the form of an informal loan to cover any expenses while you are waiting for the cheque to arrive.

Loans

The government set up the Student Loan Company back in 1990, and although it was a controversial move at the time, the Student Loan Scheme is now hugely popular with starving students everywhere. All students on higher education courses of an undergraduate degree or equivalent and students studying the Postgraduate Certificate of Education are eligible to apply.

The rate of interest is very low and the maximum amount you can borrow each year is designed to make up for the cuts to grant levels. You can take out a loan each year you are studying but the amount available is reduced in your final year because, to all intents and purposes, you will only be a student until June of that year. The amount is also slightly reduced if you live away from home but could reasonably commute to college. Since it was set up, the Student Loan Company has lent millions of pounds to students and, although there have been many problems, most students find their loan a vital source of financial support.

You cannot apply for a loan until after you have arrived at college. Every college and university has a student loan office and to apply for the student loan you have to fill in an eligibility form and take along proof of your bank account number and sort code (on your cheque book usually), your birth certificate (or your passport) and your letter from the local education authority about your award for fees. The eligibility form is then assessed and if you fit the bill you can fill out a loan application form and state how much you want to borrow. If you apply at the beginning of the academic year you can ask to have the loan paid in three instalments at the start of each term. If you apply at any other time you can have only one payment and, should you decide to borrow less than the maximum loan, you can't make another application later in the year. Then the Student Loan Company will send you a formal loan agreement (stating all the terms and conditions of the loan) and a direct debit form. Once you've signed both and sent them off to the Student Loan Company, the loan will be paid directly into your bank account.

Unfortunately, unlike grants, the loan does have to be paid back, but repayment doesn't begin until the April after you graduate or leave college. If you are unemployed then or earning less than a certain amount (eighty-five per cent of the national average earnings), you can apply to defer repayment, but interest will still be clocking up. If you don't defer repayment, the Student Loan Company will simply deduct the amount you owe straight out of your bank account each month for five years. If, for some reason, you default on repayment, by closing down your bank account or refusing to pay, the Student Loan Company will take you to court to get the money back.

Benefits

Most students are not eligible for state benefits during the time they are studying, although there are some exceptions for student parents with a dependent child and for some students with disabilities. Other exceptions are students under the age of nineteen following a further education course but not a higher education course and pensioners who meet the conditions for Income Support.

Access Funds

The government gives each college and university an amount of money to use as access funds. The principle behind access funds is that they are a limited supply of grants which the college can spend to increase access to education and according to this principle, the money could be used to increase access for student parents or for students with disabilities. But in practice the money is used in most cases to make one-off extra grants to students in hardship. Every college has an access fund office and, if you are concerned that you won't have enough money to live on, you should apply as soon as you can after arriving at college. The funds are really in demand and the grants run out fast. Most colleges will not give out access funds to students who haven't applied for the student loan, but each college works to its own rules on how to distribute their access funds.

Alternative Financial Assistance

Alternative ways of finding assistance are very limited indeed. However, there are a number of educational charities and trusts which may be able to help. They usually have quite specific and even unusual terms which students must satisfy to be eligible. For example, they may be interested only in students studying a particular course, or students from a particular area in the country, or of a certain age, or training for certain professions or for certain industries.

You may also try to apply for sponsorship or a bursary, but again the opportunities are very limited. The Careers and Occupational Information Centre produces a booklet, *Sponsorship for Students*, which lists all the scholarships and bursaries available for courses. Details of the Careers and Occupational Information Centre are available from the Department for Education and

Employment. There may be more forms of assistance available from private businesses and charitable trusts but the competition will be tough. The *Educational Grants Directory* published by the Directory of Social Change is a useful source of leads, and for engineering students the booklet *Sponsorship and Training Opportunities in Engineering*, published by the Institute of Mechanical Engineering, is worth getting hold of.

Getting a Bank Account

Your bank manager is likely to become one of your greatest pen-pals over the course of your student life, the source not only of more funds, but also of much strife if things go wrong and of much comfort when things go right. Keeping on the right side of your bank manager is easy enough, but in order to do so you will have to keep an eye on your balance and keep in regular contact.

Getting a bank account is easy. The High Street banks and building societies are falling over themselves in a rush to push for new student customers. Free pizzas, cinema vouchers and cash incentives are among the glittering prizes on offer, as well as interest-free overdrafts, credit cards, cheque books and cheque guarantee cards. There are also special deals for traveller's cheques for students and some banks also offer insurance. Shop around for the best deals in terms of overdrafts and don't be lured by the freebies and fancy gifts.

The best bank for you may well be different from that of your class-mates. Some students opt for the bank with the branch nearest to their campus, others prefer to stay with the same bank as their parents as this makes it easier for parents to transfer funds into their account and the bank may be eager to please to keep the family's custom. Having a branch on or near campus usually means there will be specially trained student banking advisers, who are more than familiar with the trials and tribulations of students' money problems and may be more sympathetic than a suburban branch. The decision, in the end, is all yours. But remember that it is possible to change banks and these days most banks will happily take on a transfer of your account, overdraft and all. Their plan is that one day you will make it rich, with your debit balance sliding into credit once you are on a salary. Then they can offer you a mortgage, a loan for a car and a savings scheme and make some serious money out of you.

If you already have a bank account you should inform your bank in writing that you would like to change it into a student account. For formality's sake you may be asked to fill in the appropriate forms for a student account and you will be asked to produce evidence of your new status as a student. This will guarantee your special preferential treatment – free overdrafts and usually a cash gift or some other incentive, as well as access to student banking advisers, who can help should you run into financial problems later.

If you are opening an account for the first time, you will need to take along some form of formal identification – your passport, birth certificate or driving licence, for example – and proof of your student status, such as the letter from your local education authority, your college acceptance letter, grant cheque or student identity card if you have already registered. The application form is fairly straightforward. It usually takes three or four days for your application to be processed, and then your cheque guarantee card, cheque book and code for using the cashpoint (your PIN number) will be sent to you separately. If you are planning to open an account after you have enrolled at college, it is a good idea to make sure you take enough cash with you to cover any expenses while you are waiting for your application to be processed.

Your bank may well include a Switch or Visa Delta card with your cheque guarantee and cashpoint card. These are debit cards and quite different from credit cards. You can use them to pay for things without having to write out a cheque but the money comes out of your account a few days later, whereas credit cards allow you to run up debts which you are asked to pay back each month or to pay back just a proportion of the balance and then pay interest on the remainder. Debit cards just take the money straight out of your account and most students find them a useful way to pay, but you will have to take care to watch how much you spend. If you pay by cheque, you can fill in the cheque-book stubs and keep a careful watch on your balance. If you pay by debit card, you should keep the receipts and work out how much is going out of your account.

Once your account is up and running the bank will send you a statement each month, listing all the transactions into and out of your account. Read it through carefully and make sure it tallies with your cheque-book stubs and cashpoint receipts. If you need a statement earlier you can request one through the cashpoint or you can pop into the bank and ask for one. You will still get your monthly statement sent through at the usual time in the month but you might find it helpful to watch your account more often. You can also get a balance of your account from the cashpoint or over the counter in the bank.

Credit Cards

Some banks offer students the option of taking out credit cards and will usually offer students a slightly cheaper rate of interest than they do for their other customers. But be wary. Credit cards are an incredibly expensive way to borrow money and it is easy to run up huge debts. Unless you pay the balance off in full each month, the interest will quickly add up. Credit cards have their uses, especially if you are likely to travel abroad, but they can be dangerous unless you budget really carefully and make sure you have enough money to pay off the balance each month. If you fail to make any payment at the end of each month, the credit card company will charge you extra interest and you could end up with a bad credit rating, which could mean they withdraw your card and even try to take you to court. It could also affect your credit rating for the future, making it difficult for you to take out loans or to get further credit cards long after you have graduated.

Overdrafts and Borrowing from Banks

Most students use the interest-free overdrafts the banks offer. It is virtually impossible to balance your books, even if you get a full grant and take out a student loan, and many students find the interest-free overdraft a life-saver towards the end of each term. Even though the interest-free overdrafts on offer can be up to as much as £1,000, many students find they sometimes need to borrow more. It is not unusual for students to run up debts with the bank of more than £2,000, and the banks offer special low rates of interest to students borrowing over the interest-free amount. The important thing to remember is that you should never go overdrawn or over your overdraft limit without permission. Check your bank balance as often as you can, and keep a running tab on how much you have in your account, and contact the bank as soon as you can if you think you might need to take out an overdraft or extend your current overdraft limit.

The best way to apply for an overdraft or an extension to your overdraft is by letter. Address your letter to the bank manager or your personal student banking adviser if you have been given one, and explain politely that despite diligent budgeting you will need to borrow more money, and state clearly how much you will need. The bank is unlikely to have a problem with agreeing to your request – in fact most banks expect students to borrow money, so there's no reason to worry so long as you give the bank enough notice.

Here is an example of a letter to the bank manager:

Date

Bank manager's name
Address of bank

Dear Mr/Ms . . .

Student account number: . . .

I would like to arrange an overdraft (or extension to my present overdraft limit) to cover my account. Unfortunately I have to pay out next term's hall fees and buy more course books in the next few weeks and will need extra funds to cover these expenses.

Please could you let me know as soon as possible if you could arrange to give me an overdraft/extend my overdraft limit by £500, and let me know of the interest rates and terms which might apply.

Thank you so much for you help.

Yours sincerely
(signed)
Your name
Your address

If you do go overdrawn or over your limit without permission you will find it will cost you dearly. The bank will charge you for sending you a letter informing you that you are overdrawn. This usually costs in the region of £15 per letter. They will charge you a high rate of interest on the amount you have overspent and, of course, interest on the charges for the letters telling you that you are overdrawn. If you have written any cheques without your guarantee card, for example your rent cheque or a cheque made out to a friend, these will not be honoured, and not only will they bounce but you will be charged around £20 for every cheque that bounces. If you have any standing orders or direct debits going out of your account these will not be processed. The Annual Percentage Rate (APR) of interest on unauthorized borrowing can be as much as thirty per cent.

Getting into Debt

Getting into financial problems is par for the course for today's students. But it is important that you seek help as soon as you can. Money problems can cause enormous stress and it could affect your health and your performance at college. Don't hide your head in the sand, go out and get help. Students are lucky in that there are quite a few places they can go to for advice on money problems and you may find that, as well as constructive advice on budgeting and getting your debt under control, you may be eligible for special hardship loans or grants. Don't be embarrassed about being in debt. These days, being a student and being in debt is as common as having an overdue library book.

Bank
As well as specially trained student banking advisers, there will be other members of staff at your bank who can offer advice and help sort out your financial problems and you may be surprised at how sympathetic banks can be towards students. Write or phone and make an appointment to visit a banking adviser or the bank manager and talk through your worries and your needs with them. They may be willing to waive some of the interest or charges you have run up and can offer advice on limiting your spending, as well as sorting out or extending your overdraft.

Student Union
All student unions have welfare advisers and student counsellors, who deal with students with financial problems every day. You may have to make an appointment or you may be able just to drop in. Many student unions have set up special hardship funds to

help students who are in real problems and they may offer you a short-term loan or even a grant to help you through a difficult patch.

Tutors and College Student Counsellors

Your college will employ student counsellors, and you may also turn to your personal tutor for help. They may be able to advise you of any special schemes available at your college. It is best to let your tutor know if you are having problems as they will take this into consideration when assessing your college work. You will find them very sympathetic and helpful.

Budgeting

Even if you get a full grant it is unlikely to cover as much as half of your expenditure. As well as rent, travel and food, there are books to buy and a multitude of daily outgoings. It is the little things that add up. Money is going to be very tight and the only way to keep debt in control is to budget and to watch your spending carefully.

One of the main problems facing students trying to manage their money is the fact that money arrives in one lump sum at the start of term and it can be difficult working out spending limits for the week and for the month. If you live in a hall of residence you will usually pay your rent in one payment for the whole term, but in other accommodation you may find you pay your rent each month. It will also be difficult to assess exactly how much you will be needing to spend each week. The first few weeks at college are hectic and expensive. Books, signing up for clubs and societies, and buying drinks at the daily freshers' social events all cost money, but won't be regular expenditures every week. You may find you spend more in the first few weeks than you will later on in the term.

Once you have worked out how much money you are going to get in terms of grant and loan, the next step is to work out how much you are going to have to spend each term and each week, and how much you may have to borrow or earn to make ends meet.

Draw up a budget with an estimate of your income and outgoings for the term ahead, and work out your priorities. Necessary expenditure like rent, food, travel, insurance and fuel bills will be the major outgoings. These are things you just can't go without. Defaulting on your rent or bills or running out of money for food or travel can cause real problems and you need to make sure you have covered these necessities before you splash out on a night out, a new pair of shoes or a special treat.

Rent will almost certainly be the biggest expenditure. For many students, rent takes up almost all their grant. Some halls of residence cost more than the total maximum grant. If you live in halls it may also include the cost of some meals and a contribution towards fuel bills. Otherwise you will be spending a considerable amount on fuel bills, which are usually paid each quarter. Food is going to be your next big expenditure and is something you cannot go without. As well as eating breakfast and dinner at home, you will have to buy lunch or take your lunch with you.

Travel, to and from college and back to your family home or to visit friends, can be another big part of your spending, but you can save money by investing in discount travel cards. Both National Express coaches and British Rail run discount schemes for students and young people, offering as much as a third off the normal ticket price – an absolute must if you are planning to travel around the country visiting friends and family – and you will probably save the initial outlay within the first few trips. For day-to-day travelling it will probably make sense to buy a season ticket, rather than paying out the full ticket price every day. In some towns and cities the local bus companies offer discounts for students. If such a scheme is not already up and running, you could always talk to your student union about negotiating a student discount with them. Day-to-day travelling is a major part of most students' weekly expenditure and, not surprisingly, many turn to pedal power to save money on bus and train tickets. The initial investment on a bike need not break the bank either. It is possible to pick up second-hand bikes for next to nothing and, in the long term, this might be better than splashing out on the latest top-of-the-range bicycle, which may be stolen.

You will also need to get insurance. Insurance is essential – even if you feel your possessions aren't worth that much. Should they get stolen or damaged, it will cost much more to replace them than it does to pay out your insurance premiums annually. Student accommodation is notoriously prone to theft and whether you are staying in privately rented accommodation or a college hall of residence there is a real risk of your prized possessions running away with the local thief. There are many places offering student insurance deals, including banks and separate insurance companies. Endsleigh Insurance is the official student insurance company as it is partly owned by the National Union of Students. Endsleigh offers specially discounted student insurance packages, covering everything from computers and TVs, to bikes and travel insurance, and it has branches on most campuses.

Then you can work out how much you will be able to spend on books, going out, clothes and other luxuries. It will also help if you can break down your budget to a monthly spending basis, and limit your spending on going out and food to a reasonable amount. You don't want to starve yourself and you certainly don't want to waste your college years staying in every single night, but you will have to be careful.

It can be quite scary drawing up a budget, especially when it seems you will never be able to balance your outgoings over your income even if you borrow up to your limit. The trick is to keep your spending on all those non-essential items to a minimum, cutting corners where you can with a bit of wheeling and dealing.

- Buy food from markets – it's much cheaper than supermarkets and corner shops. Other household items, like bin-liners and toilet rolls, are also cheaper from street markets. Fresh fruit and vegetables are not only fresher they are also cheaper than tinned or frozen produce from the supermarket.
- Look out for special bulk-buy deals (for things like tea bags and toilet rolls) and check out the food on special offer at the end of the

Budget Plan

INCOME

grant	£ _____
loan	_____
support from family	_____
part-time job	_____
other	_____
Total monthly income	_____

EXPENDITURE

rent	_____
food	_____
insurance	_____
travel to college	_____
bills	_____
phone	_____
TV licence	_____
TV rental	_____
books	_____
magazines/newspapers	_____
cinema/theatre/clubs/concerts	_____
drinking out	_____
meals out	_____
sports	_____
toiletries	_____
cigarettes	_____
clothes	_____
sundries – like laundry	_____
travel home or to visit friends	_____
Total outgoings each month	_____

BALANCE = monthly income less monthly outgoings = _____

day in supermarkets. You can always chip in with friends to bulk buy if you feel you might not quite get through two hundred tea bags in one term.
- Draw up a sensible list of what you need to buy whenever you go out food shopping. Plan your meals in advance and buy only what you need. Never, ever, go food shopping when you are hungry – you will end up with all sorts of expensive snacks and goodies in your shopping bag. Have a sandwich or fill up on toast before you hit the shops.
- Don't buy pre-packed ready-to-eat meals. These work out at nearly four times the cost of making the meal yourself from basic ingredients – and if you cook up larger portions, you can save some to eat for the next day, or share with friends.
- A lot of students are vegetarian, and even if you are not inclined to a meat-free diet you might find that buying meat to eat daily proves a little too expensive. Stock up on bulk staples, like pasta, rice and potatoes to fill you up, but make sure you get plenty of the right vitamins and minerals in your diet. Living on just toast is bound to lead to malnutrition of some sort. See the section on health and happiness for tips on balancing your diet, and have a look at the recipes on pages 34–40 for ideas on cheap, cheerful but nourishing meals.
- Shop around for cheap toiletries – don't buy name brands but buy stores' own brands instead. Tampons, shampoo, soap and cotton wool are much cheaper if you buy the store's own make and you will find they are virtually the same product as the big name brand with the fancy name and expensive packaging.
- Get just a set limit out of the cashpoint each week and try not to get any extra cash out. When you are going out for the night, set a realistic limit, leaving you enough for a couple of drinks, your cinema ticket or ticket into a club and enough to get home safely. It can be tempting to spend everything in your purse and rush to the cashpoint for the next instant fix but this is where you lose control.
- If you have fuel bills to pay, try to sort out paying in instalments by direct debit in advance. This helps you to budget over the

months and weeks rather than for every three months, and saves the shock of a horrendous bill every quarter. Most of the fuel companies encourage students to pay by instalments and the electricity companies are now encouraging students to have key meters. This can help a great deal as you charge up the key whenever you need to and means you are paying for electricity in simple £10 amounts. But watch out that you don't end up running out of charged-up keys and spending an evening in the dark.

- If you really, really want that new dress, or you've set your heart on a pair of shoes, hold back. Wait at least a week and reason out your decision. Impulse shopping is the route of evil when it comes to balancing a budget. Wait and see if you still want the same thing next week and work out whether you really, really need it.
- Cut down on those little things that cost so much, like chocolate bars, cigarettes and snacks when you are out. If you are buying a sandwich out every day, and a bar of chocolate and a packet of cigarettes, you are saying goodbye to the best part of £30 a week, which could certainly be put to better use elsewhere in the essential budget headings – like rent or buying food to cook and eat at home. Buying your own bread and making up sandwiches to take into college is a whole lot cheaper than having shop-made sandwiches. A whole loaf of bread costs about a third of the price of a shop-made sandwich.
- Evenings out in your student union bar or student union disco are going to be about half the price of a night on the town. Cheaper drinks and cheap or free entry to gigs, concerts and club nights are all perks of being a student, and the student union circuit is home to the best new acts going. You might feel like you need to get out and see some 'normal' people every now and again but be prepared to pay over the odds compared with what you can get on campus.
- Student shops on campus offer real deals on stationery and other things you are likely to need for your course. Stock up on pens, paper and folders here rather than paying extra in town.

- Shop around for real bargains. If you have to buy books see if you can get them second-hand. Most colleges run book sales and nearby second-hand bookshops are likely to stock academic books. Check out notice-boards in your department for students from years before who might be selling their course books. But before you buy any book try the library. If your college library is out of stock, try the local municipal library. It may be possible for them to order the book from another branch if they don't have it in stock.
- Discounts are a blessing for all students. It is possible to get student discounts on virtually everything these days, simply by flashing your student identity card. TV rental, insurance, books, cinemas, theatres, supermarkets, record shops, clothes shops, travel companies, night-clubs, art galleries, museums, book shops, stationers' and a whole range of other businesses offer student discounts from around ten per cent off their usual rate. They figure you will become a regular customer if they can entice you in to spend money while you are still a student. Ask for details of local student discount schemes at your student union or look out for details of the special deals negotiated by the National Union of Students.
- Invest in a Young Person's Railcard from British Rail, available to all young people aged between sixteen and twenty-five and for all students, for savings of up to a third off train fares. Or if you would rather travel by bus, the National Express Discount Coach Card offers similar savings on coach travel all over the UK.

Eating on the Cheap

Even though you are living on the brink of bankruptcy you might want to cheer up your friends with a bit of a meal every now and again. Eating out is always going to be more expensive than eating in, and, with the minimum of fuss and at the cost of a fiver, you can rustle up a decent-sized dinner and impress your friends with your culinary skills.

Ellie, from York University, says making a meal for friends is a recipe for success when it comes to sorting out a good night out. 'We all get together to cook and we chop, slice, grill and simmer in the kitchen over a few glasses of cheap plonk, then we all sit down and get stuck in. Friends usually bring round a bottle of cheap wine and we get a bit giggly and enjoy a really good meal. If you shop around for ingredients you can still whisk up a fairly fancy meal without spending too much money. It is much cheaper than going out for a pizza or spending the night in the pub and we get to have those really good, late-night chats. I love having dinner parties, and I always thought I would only do them when I was properly grown-up and serving sherry, like my mother. But students can have dinner parties too, and it can be so much fun when you have good food and good company.'

Pick up fresh ingredients at the market, with extra bargains to be had in the late afternoon as the market begins to pack up. These recipes will suffice for four hungry people and make for a memorable meal without breaking your bank manager's heart. Pasta is the student staple, so we've included two deliciously cheap pasta sauces to accompany the old favourite.

Tangy tomato pasta sauce

This is very easy to make in a little time with basic ingredients you probably already have in your cupboard.

1 large tin of peeled plum tomatoes
½ large onion, sliced finely
1 clove of garlic, chopped or crushed
olive oil
Tabasco
Worcester sauce
tomato ketchup
salt
pepper

sugar

enough pasta for four people

grated Parmesan or fresh Cheddar cheese to sprinkle on top and maybe fresh basil

Sauté the onion in olive oil and add the crushed garlic after about 3 minutes, then sauté for another minute or so. Add the peeled tomatoes and stir vigorously to break them up. Then let it simmer for about 5 minutes. Add salt, pepper, a dash of Tabasco, a dash of Worcester sauce, a dash of tomato ketchup and a pinch of sugar. Stir again and then let it simmer for another 15–20 minutes. Taste and add more seasoning if you want. Meanwhile the pasta should have been simmering away for 8 minutes, depending on the quantity. Check that the pasta isn't getting too soft and, if it's cooking faster than the sauce, take it off the heat until just before you're ready to serve. Drain the pasta, place into serving bowls, add the sauce and sprinkle over the top freshly grated Parmesan or Cheddar cheese and fresh basil if you have any.

Fresh pesto sauce

This simple sauce is delicious with pasta and is much tastier and cheaper than the ready-made versions. The biggest expense is the fresh Parmesan available in supermarkets for a fraction of the price they sell it for in the delicatessen. Look out for basil on the vegetable stalls in the market. They don't always have it on display as prominently as potatoes, so you might have to ask. If you haven't invested in a blender you should put it at the top of your Christmas list. They are relatively cheap to buy and are great for making soups and sauces. If you can't lay your hands on a blender you can crush the ingredients together with a pestle and mortar. To roast the pine nuts, sprinkle them on a baking tray and put them in the top of a hot oven for a few minutes until they start to go golden.

2 good sized bags of fresh basil
a little salt
a little pepper
1 clove of garlic, crushed
pine nuts, slightly roasted – you'll need about 30 nuts altogether
olive oil
2–3 tablespoons of hot water
freshly grated Parmesan

Blend the basil, salt, pepper, garlic, pine nuts, and olive oil until reasonably smooth. Stir in finely grated Parmesan and hot water and blend again. And, hey presto, it's finished. Serve with pasta. You can store any leftovers in the fridge for up to about five days, and you can add a spoonful to soups and sauces to make them really tasty.

Mediterranean bake

This is so easy to cook and amazingly cheap, especially if you buy the vegetables from the market.

olive oil
1 large onion, chopped
2 lb courgettes, chopped
2 lb tomatoes, chopped
2 cloves of garlic, chopped
grated fresh Parmesan or strong Cheddar
salt and pepper

Heat some olive oil in a large saucepan, add the chopped onion, cover and cook on a low heat for 5 minutes or so, then add the chopped courgettes, chopped tomatoes and garlic, then stir, cover and cook for another 5 minutes. Take off the heat, stir again and add salt and pepper. Then put the whole lot into a low gratin dish or roasting tray and put under a hot grill, sprinkling the cheese on top. Grill for 5 or 6 minutes until the whole thing is bubbling and the cheese is going crispy. Serve with salad and some French bread.

Moules marinière

This is such an easy meal to cook, and mussels (moules) are really cheap if you buy them from the fish stall in the market. It is best served with lots of fresh French bread.

1 big bag of mussels (about 60 big mussels)
1 onion
2 oz butter
half a bottle of dry white wine
chopped parsley
black pepper
one very large pan with a lid – to fit in all the mussels

First clean the mussels by washing them in cold running water and scrub the shells with a small nail brush to get rid of all the bits of stringy fluff and grit. Leave to soak in cold water for an hour or so. Then chop up the onion and cook it in the butter in the big pan until it's golden. Add the white wine and seasoning and bring to simmering point, then add the mussels, cover and leave for 6 minutes or so. The wine sauce will bubble up and cover the mussels and the steam will open up the mussel shells. When the shells have all opened, spoon the mussels into bowls, pour the sauce over the top of each bowl to cover the mussels and sprinkle on the chopped parsley. If any of the shells have failed to open you should just throw them away.

Normandy pork

This is a dish for extra-special occasions, but ever so easy. You will have to ask at the butcher's or meat stall in the market to get the pork medallions.

1 large onion
groundnut oil
4 pork medallions
a big glug of brandy
fresh cream
salt and pepper
chopped parsley

Sauté the onion in the oil until soft and add the pork medallions. The medallions need about 4 minutes on each side. Add the brandy and then light with a match. Burn off the alcohol, then add the fresh cream. Season with salt and pepper, and carry on cooking for about 5 minutes, until the pork is completely tender. Serve garnished with fresh parsley and the vegetables of your choice.

Roasted red pepper and tomato dressing

This is a delicious dressing for either pasta or a mixed leaf salad.

2 red peppers
4 tomatoes
olive oil
1 clove of garlic, crushed
sugar
salt and pepper
fresh basil

Roast the red peppers and the tomatoes in the oven for about 25 minutes, drizzled with olive oil. Their skins will go black and blistered. Take them out of the oven and peel the skins off carefully, using a sharp knife and your fingers. Then blend together the peeled tomatoes and peppers, adding a big splodge of olive oil, the crushed garlic, a sprinkle of sugar, salt, pepper and fresh basil.

You can add paprika, chilli or cayenne pepper to give it an extra kick.

Chocolate fudge cake

This is a gorgeous cake and relatively cheap and easy to make. Once you've bought the ingredients you can store them in the cupboard till the next time you want to make the cake, so the initial outlay on flour and sugar isn't as bad as it seems. You can make just the chocolate fudge sauce – it's delicious with bananas or ice cream.

For the cake:
6 oz self-raising flour
6 oz caster sugar
6 oz soft margarine
2 eggs
half a cup of milk
1 teaspoon baking powder
lots of cocoa powder

Throw the lot in a mixing bowl and stir up together until they form the perfect cake mix. Keep tasting and add more cocoa powder until you are satisfied that it's really chocolatey. Add more milk if it seems to be a bit too dry. Then place into two greased, round sandwich tins in the middle of an oven, preheated to 190°C for about 20 minutes. Keep checking so they don't burn and use a knife to test whether they are cooked all the way through: stick the knife in and it should come out clean. If it's still gooey inside, keep it in the oven for another 5 minutes or so. When cooked, leave to cool for 5 minutes and then turn out on to plates to cool thoroughly. Don't stack them on top of each other yet or they may stick.

For the chocolate fudge sauce:
3 oz granulated sugar
1–2 oz of butter or margarine
4 oz of cooking chocolate or ordinary chocolate
4 fl oz of evaporated milk (about two-thirds of a small tin)
vanilla essence (optional)

Put the milk and sugar in a saucepan and, on a low heat, stir carefully to dissolve all the sugar. This can take a few minutes. When the sugar has dissolved (the scratchy feel disappears), bring to the boil and watch carefully not to let it burn or boil over, then turn the heat right down and simmer for about 6 minutes. You have to keep watching to make sure it doesn't boil or burn but keeps bubbling. Then take from the heat, add the chocolate and stir until it melts into the mix. Add the margarine and stir it in, then add a few drops of vanilla essence, if you have any. Transfer to a bowl and put in the fridge for a few hours. Then, when it's cool and set, you can spread it between a sandwich of the two cakes and on top of the cake. You can ice the cake with melted chocolate if you find you've used up all the fudge on the inside.

The cake will keep in the fridge for a few days for a tasty snack after a long day of lectures!

Fashion on a Shoestring

Fashion on the cheap is the canny student's solution to the sort of sartorial challenges caused by living on a shoestring. It is possible to look good for next to nothing. Most of the time you can get away with cardigans, Sloppy Joe jumpers, jeans and leggings, and for day-to-day wear you can't really go wrong with these. You can pick these staples up in the markets and you will probably find they cost half the price they do in the shops. Check out all the local second-hand and charity shops for accessories and extras. The retro look is very much in on campus and anything which looks forties, fifties, sixties or seventies will add some street style to your outfit.

Jumble sales are another good source of high fashion on a low budget. Clare, a student in London, keeps up with the pressure to look cool in the capital by finding hidden treasures at local jumbles. 'We check out the local paper for ads for jumbles coming up in school halls and churches. They are usually on a Saturday morning and the trick is to turn up as early as possible and to be prepared to haggle. I have found some brilliant things recently. Little twin sets, tight cardigans, and a big sloppy jumper. The knitwear is the best. I don't know why people throw out these things that are basically perfect. I've also picked up a great Harris tweed jacket for 50p, a mock plastic jacket which is very modish for £2, and a forties-style snap-shut handbag which is brilliant for going out. I take care to wash all the woollen things thoroughly but you can't just throw them in the hot wash as they come out a few sizes smaller. I try not to buy things that will need dry cleaning but I got the tweed jacket dry cleaned, though this meant the total cost of this very trendy item was £3.50 in the end, which is still a real bargain. I love going to jumbles. It is a good laugh and you can come back with sackfuls of goodies without spending more than a few pounds. I've had shirts for 10p which I've only worn a few times but it doesn't really matter when they cost half the price of a phone call to my mum.'

From time to time you might be required to dress up a bit, and keeping up with the gin-and-tonic GTi set is never as easy without their bank balances. But there's an art in being crafty and you can end up looking more original than the designer-labelled ball belles.

Angela, a second-year at Cambridge, explains, 'There are so many parties and balls to go to. Everyone else seems to have more money, flashier clothes, designer labels even. At first I really panicked that I was going to look fairly dowdy in my one little black dress from the chain store that I'd had since the sixth form. But it is amazing what you can do to jazz things up with very little cash. I bought a length of feather boa from a haberdashery stall in the market, some cheap and nasty earrings from a chain store, and picked up some arm-length black satin gloves from a second-hand shop, and with my little black dress I looked just as good as anyone else. In fact I probably looked a lot better than the Laura Ashley taffeta clones who turn up at all the balls. But it is an outfit which has served me fine through a few balls and parties now and needs just a few variations to keep it going a while more. I have a friend who has been stunning the crowds at the Cambridge balls with a satin slip she picked up at a charity shop. It is actually a nylon nightie but it has little spaghetti straps and looks for all the world like satin and it really does her proud.'

Thrift-store chic is the buzz word on campus and finding something really original at a fraction of the price of the big shops is not as hard as it seems. Much of the stuff you can pick up at jumbles and charity shops can be adapted, taken in, taken up and transformed with a few stitches. Oxfam set up a project with fashion design students and launched the Oxfam No Logo shops which have opened up recently. Here you can pick up Oxfam's best donations which have been revamped by fashion students into some of the trendiest and most original stuff, and still have change for the bus fare home.

Two big chain stores, Top Shop and Miss Selfridge, offer students ten per cent discount with their NUS card. They can be great for leggings, T-shirts and skimpy dresses which can be tarted up for special occasions with cheap and trendy junk jewellery. You can also get the same discount on shoes at Top Shop and Miss Selfridge, which is probably better for your feet than trying to hammer them into some second-hand 50s stilettos.

If you can still remember the basics from school needlework lessons, you might want to try running up a few things yourself. Patterns are incredibly cheap, and fabric from the market can be bought for just a few pounds. Check out the books of patterns in sewing shops or the sewing section of your local department store.

You usually get a few designs with each pattern, leaving you with the opportunity to produce a few variations on a theme. Choose something simple if you're not up to much as a seamstress, then beg, borrow or steal your relation's ancient sewing machine to run up a brand new, latest design, very original item all by yourself. You can alternatively ask your mum to do it for you, but that would be cheating.

Sophie, a student at Bath, says rustling up a few frocks on her mum's old machine has saved her a great deal of money over the past year and won her a few Brownie points in style. 'I was never really that good at sewing but whenever I go home for the holidays or even just for the weekend I take along a simple pattern and some material and whizz up a shift dress, a wrap-around-skirt or some draw-string trousers. The patterns you can get are really trendy and you don't have to go for the fancy-frills-and-difficult-cuffs-and-sleeves jobs they try and make you do at school. I've expanded my wardrobe three times over in the past year and I shouldn't think I've spent more than £20 on material. It is much easier than you think.'

Getting a Job

You might find the best way to raise enough money to keep you in the black, or at least within the safe limits of red, will be to take on a part-time job. More and more students are finding this the only way to survive and around ten per cent of students now work more than twenty hours a week, on top of their studies. Wherever you go about town or on campus you will find students working in pubs and pizza parlours, in the cinema or sports centre, or in the student union bar. Part-time work has become part and parcel of student life. *Cosmo*'s latest survey found three-quarters of students have a part-time job.

Having a part-time job is not just a good thing because of the extra funds it brings in. You can also pick up valuable CV points in terms of experience and, of course, if you are out working, you will be saving the money you would be spending if you were going out instead.

If your course includes a work placement or if you have the opportunity to do some work experience, you may be able to apply for a National Vocational Qualification (NVQ), which would be based on your performance at work rather than on your sitting an exam. By achieving an NVQ, you will obviously be in a stronger position when it comes to the job hunt.

Juggling a job with your studies can be hard work in itself. All too easily, study time can be sacrificed for the sake of a pay packet and, unless you are careful to keep time set aside for study, you will find your academic work will suffer, especially if your part-time work is tiring. But it is not impossible to combine work and study and a social life. It just takes a fair amount of organization and discipline. It is important to remember the real reason why you came to college and to prioritize your essays and exams where necessary. Colleges and universities have accepted the fact that most students need to take on jobs these days, and are much more lenient than they used to be about the impact this has on study time. Many student unions have now set up job centres and job notice-boards to help students find work.

Part-time jobs are not always easy to come by, and recent research by the National Union of Students found that twenty per cent of students wanted to work but could not find a job. Most part-time job vacancies go in the first few weeks of term and, especially in areas of high unemployment, students are competing with the local unemployed for vacancies. Unfortunately most students cannot be as flexible as to when they can work because of college timetabling, lectures and their obvious need to take time off for exams and revision. If you want to get a job you will need a lot of luck and a fair amount of persistence to find something suitable.

Finding Work

Try out college notice-boards first and check if your student union runs a job centre or job notice-board. Student unions employ big numbers of student staff to work behind the bars, to work as security at events, in the student shops and cafés, as DJs, swimming-pool attendants and in all their other outlets and operations, so it is well worth enquiring after possible vacancies on campus first. This has the double benefit of being flexible employment with a safe and responsible employer and at the same time keeping you in contact with the student community. The student unions pay competitive rates of pay to student staff and generally treat student staff very well.

Jobs off campus are harder to come by, and some Job Centres in towns actually discourage students from enquiring after vacancies as their priority is to find jobs for the local unemployed. Most students find work off campus by word-of-mouth and by making casual enquiries. Pubs, clubs, bars, restaurants, shops and cafés are the best places to try, and experience is never essential. Put on something vaguely tidy and a cheery disposition and ask to speak to the manager about possible vacancies. For the big High Street chain shops and some restaurant and pub chains, you might be asked to fill in an application form and accept a place on the waiting list. It is best to try as many places as possible and to put yourself on as many waiting lists as you can.

If you have basic typing skills you might try approaching a temping agency. With higher rates of pay than shop or bar work, temping agencies accept students on their books and will give you a call when and if they get a suitable day's work. It won't be regular work but it will pay well, and you might find the chance to impress possible future employers. A chance day's work filing in an advertising agency or PR company might give you an insight into an area of work which might interest you as a future career and can be an opportunity to make useful contacts to call on when you graduate.

As well as the temping agencies that deal with clerical work, such as typing, filing, reception work and data entry, there are temping agencies which specialize in placing casual staff in other areas of work, such as catering and factory work, so you might want to consider getting your name on their books. Many of these agencies will be able to help with finding blocks of work over the summer and it might be useful for you to get yourself registered and in the front running for the much sought-after summer jobs. For temping jobs which require a level of skill or expertise, such as silver-service waiting, expect a higher rate of pay than you would get employed directly by a restaurant or bar, but again the risk is that this work is not usually regular and may not give you the guaranteed earnings you need to make ends meet.

The really wily student will do her best to find a part-time job which will get her some useful experience for her future career as well as earning some extra money to see her through college. If you have an idea of the field you would like to work in, it might be a good idea to target specific organizations and companies that work in your chosen career area. Send off a typed letter and a copy of your CV, explaining that you are a student and looking for part-time work, that you would be very interested in working in this field when you graduate and you would be happy to take on any work within their company in order to get some experience of how their industry works. Most employers will be impressed with such diligence and determination, and the practical advantages for them of having someone who is interested in their work and keen to impress will obviously affect their decision as to whether to take you on. If you don't have time to work during term-time or their company hours will not suit your own timetable of study and availability for work, you should write to them in the spring to line up possible work for the summer.

Words of Warning

Sometimes when the going gets really tough, it might be tempting to consider taking on work which could put you at risk or endanger your health. Increasing numbers of students are tempted by the lucrative work on offer with escort agencies, but you should be wary of the obvious problems this can encourage. Another, and much more dangerous, fast-buck alternative to regular part-time work is to take part in clinical testing. Student volunteers can be paid huge amounts of money to undergo medical tests for new drugs, and an estimated 25,000 students a year take part in clinical trials. But be warned: students have died after taking part in medical trials.

The temptation of giving up a short amount of time for a large amount of cash can be hard to resist, but possible side effects and long-term damage could far outweigh the material gains you could make. The National Union of Students and the Association of Clinical Research Contractors drew up guidelines for student participation in clinical trials back in the 1980s, after two students died as a result of drug tests, in a bid to protect students and to restrict the activities of cowboy companies recruiting students for potentially dangerous drug tests. If you ever consider taking part or are approached by a company asking for healthy student volunteers, you should let your student union know as soon as possible and make sure the procedure of the company concerned is consistent with the NUS guidelines. If you do decide to take the risk you at least owe it to yourself to check the company involved is a legitimate practitioner and to be as informed as possible on any likely side effects. Check with your doctor before you agree to any tests and don't rely solely on the medical the company should give you before you take part.

Tax and National Insurance

If you are earning money you may find you are eligible to pay National Insurance and income tax on your earnings, but not necessarily.

Income tax is calculated as a percentage of your earnings after a deduction of your personal allowance – a sum set each year in the government's budget which is basically tax-free. Grants and most other educational scholarships are exempt from tax so this is not included in any calculation of your earnings. The personal allowance is calculated according to your circumstances: there is a set rate for single people, a rate for married couples and a rate for a single parent who looks after a child. The single person's personal allowance currently stands at £3,445. Basically you will not pay tax at all so long as your annual earnings do not exceed that sum.

Tax is paid in one of two ways, either as you are paid so that it is automatically deducted (Pay As You Earn, or PAYE as it is known) or on an assessment at the end of the tax year in April. Most part-time work, Saturday jobs or evening work during term-time are unlikely to pay you more than your personal allowance, so if you, and your employer, fill in the Inland Revenue form P38 (S) you will be exempt from tax. This form is specifically for students, and your employer should be able to get hold of one for you or you can call your local tax office. Their number will be listed in the telephone directory. You might find that vacation work, especially during the long summer vacation, might take you up to and over the threshold of your personal allowance and you may find you pay tax through PAYE on your earnings in the summer if you are working full-time through the whole summer. If, at the end of the year, the tax office find you have overpaid tax through this automatic deduction, they will refund the tax by cheque.

Students on work placements will find they have to pay tax normally, subject to their personal allowance deduction. However, any wages or salary paid to them during the time they are studying at college which would normally be taxable can be tax-free, provided the student is enrolled at the college for at least one academic year, that attendance at college is at least twenty weeks full-time within the academic year and that the level of earnings does not exceed £7,000. If you are a placement student you should get in touch with the tax office to make sure you are exempt from paying tax.

If you are earning anything over £57 a week from part-time work, or full-time work in the vacation, you should be paying National Insurance. This is deducted at source by the employer. This threshold is fixed by the government, so it can vary from year to year. Basically you will have pay two per cent on your first £57 and ten per cent on anything above that. Your employer will also have to pay out National Insurance on your behalf. Everyone is issued with a National Insurance number once they reach the age of sixteen, and you should have received a credit-card-sized piece of plastic with your number on it around your sixteenth birthday. If you lose your number or the card, you can get a replacement and you should contact your local Department of Social Security office for a new one.

Chapter 3 / **Study**

Studying at college is a million miles away from the safe routine of school days, and it is hardly surprising that most freshers are completely bewildered by the prospect. Out go the fixed timetables, homework and structured teaching, and in come tutorials, seminars, dissertations, independent study, presentations and lectures. Studying at college is about being resourceful and independent, with a fair amount of thinking for yourself and motivating yourself to do as much as you can as well as you can.

The key to success is being organized, which is no mean feat when you first arrive in your college department with an open mind and an empty diary. Choosing course options that don't clash, finding seminar rooms, signing up for lecture courses and even pinning down your tutor for some advice can be an ordeal in itself. It is your responsibility to plan your own study agenda, to sign up for courses, register for exams and organize your time to accommodate sessions in the library, in the computer centre and studying at home. The emphasis at college is on you, your decisions, your motivation and your determination to make the most of the opportunities on offer.

It is also not unusual to feel suddenly out of your depth and inadequate. You've gone from being a big fish in a little pond to being a tiny speck of plankton in the huge ocean of college life. The pressures of success and the fear of failure can be overwhelming, especially if you are weighed down by the expectations of your family and friends. Don't worry if you feel desperately lonely, worried and unhappy, because these feelings are very common for freshers and you will find your classmates will be feeling the same. You can always ask your student union welfare officer for advice or talk things through with your personal tutor. You wouldn't have made it on to the course if they didn't think you were good enough in the first place, so put thoughts of failure to the back of your mind and see the confusion as a challenge. It really won't take long to get into the swing of things.

Getting Started

Those first meetings arranged by your college department to introduce you to the course and the course tutors are crucial. It is important to pay attention to gain the maximum amount of information. Often these meetings give students an outline of what will be expected of them over the next few years, such as how many course options you will be required to pass and the schedule of exams and assessment throughout the course.

Befriending the departmental secretary or administrative assistant is also useful. The departmental secretary will not only be able to point you in the right direction of rooms and lecture theatres, but can also help with getting hold of reading lists, tutorial timetables, hand-outs you may have missed and all sorts of other information. It is also a good idea to chat to students in the years above. Most college departments have a common room or a social area for meeting and mingling or you may find that your college department organizes pairing schemes, with students from the year above paired to freshers to help them with basic information and advice in those nerve-racking first weeks.

Lots of colleges have started running study-skills courses for new students in the first semester, and it may be worth making your own enquiries about any programmes your college may put on for new recruits. These courses teach new students about note-taking in lectures, managing your time, coping with deadlines and the art and craft of independent study. It might seem over-zealous to spend time learning how to study but it will definitely pay off in the end.

College study has changed dramatically in recent years and the old structures of studying for three years and taking all the exams at the end (finals) are being phased out in favour of modularization and semesterization. These new ideas allow for students to take a number of modules over two or three semesters each year and allow more time for revision. It also means you take exams in each module at the end of each semester rather than having to cram in three years of study into two weeks of exams right at the end. Most students find this a much more flexible way of studying and it certainly relieves much of the pressure and stress faced by old-fashioned finalists. But there are still teething problems with the new systems and if you run into any difficulties, make sure your course tutor is aware.

Tutors and Tutorials

When you first arrive you will be assigned your own personal tutor. This will be an academic, a professor or a lecturer, within your college department. Their role as your personal tutor is to provide you with help and assistance, guidance and advice about your course and also to help with any personal problems you may have that might affect your performance at college, such as pointing you in the direction of hardship funds if you run out of money, or defending you in appeals over exams or in the unlikely event of you being involved in a disciplinary hearing. Should you arrive at college and find you have decided to change course, your personal tutor will be able to give you advice on how to do this and work with you to arrange it.

Your personal tutor will help you with choosing course options, supervise your study and revision and offer advice on dissertations and assessment work. They may also set you additional study and essays and, depending on the course or the college, you may have to meet with them for tutorials on a fortnightly or monthly basis. Sometimes this will be just you and the tutor but more often these days it will be you and a few other students who share your tutor. Tutorials are quite intensive study sessions, when you will be asked to develop arguments and defend your opinions on your subject, and you are usually asked to do some preparation work before the tutorial. Missing tutorials isn't a good idea. Since you are likely to be either the only student there or one of just a few, your absence will be far more noticeable than if you missed a lecture.

If, for any reason, you don't get on with your personal tutor (and it does happen) then it is relatively easy to change. The head of the department or the departmental secretary will be able to give you advice on this if you don't want to bring the matter up with your personal tutor directly, but you should find that swapping to another tutor within your department is an easy process.

Tips on Tutorials

Do any background reading that you've been set. Bluffing won't help at all: it will be obvious you don't know what you're talking about. You can only make the most of your time if you've put in the work beforehand. If you've been asked to read a whole book and managed to get only half-way through, then say so at the beginning of the tutorial and make your excuses before it's too late to get out of the hole.

Team up with others in your tutorial group to study outside of the tutorial. Even if it's just going for a coffee before or after the tutorial it will give you a good chance to develop your ideas without having the pressures of performance in front of your tutor. Photocopy each other's essays and notes to give new perspectives on the subject you have discussed. Tutorials are not competitive and you can gain a great deal from sharing an enthusiasm for your study.

If you can't make a tutorial, it is a good idea to send a short handwritten note to the tutor explaining your absence and asking for the work that has been set for the next tutorial.

If you've started falling behind on other work set by other course tutors and lecturers you should let your personal tutor know about it. Explain any problems and make your excuses so that your personal tutor will be in a position to defend you if necessary.

Your personal tutor will be the one who will defend your case if you feel you have been wrongly assessed or if your exam results are not what you've been expecting. They will also defend you in a disciplinary hearing in the rare event of you running into real trouble with the college, so it's important they know about any problems you might have. They will be experienced at dealing with all sorts of students' problems, such as homesickness or exam stress, pregnancy or poverty, family problems or relationship breakdowns, and they will offer at least a sympathetic ear if not sound advice on where to go for more help.

Lectures

With two hundred other students in a very hot or very cold dark room and always on incredibly uncomfortable chairs, you are required to sit and listen to one lone voice for nearly an hour, and by the time they get to offering to answer questions over half the students will be fast asleep. There's never a good time for a lecture. They are always too early in the day, or too late, or just before lunch or just after. But, unfortunately, they should not be missed. Often lectures are taken by lecturers from other courses and even other colleges and give you the chance to hear a topic explained by a real expert in the field. In some colleges and universities, lecturers from other colleges are occasionally beamed in via a video link on the Internet and the lecture will be shown simultaneously in several colleges on a big video screen. Because it is a two-way link, they can still see you and answer your questions.

The trick with lectures is not to write everything down. There are far too many jokes about freshers at lectures scribbling down 'Good morning'. Lectures should be treated as a briefing, an introduction to a topic or a line of thought on a subject and if only they were more visually stimulating it might be easier to listen without drifting into daydreams and even sleep. As it is, writing down key words, phrases, names of people, places and books to read up on after the lecture is the way to get the most out of the session and will keep you alert enough actually to learn. Reading up on the subject before the lecture will give you an extra interest and you may even have some questions to ask at the end. Some students take Dictaphone tape recorders into lectures, and then transcribe key points in the lecture at a later stage, but this might mean you end up relying on technology to record information for you rather than absorbing it first-hand.

Tips on Lectures

Lectures provide new angles on information you will pick up through more intensive study sessions such as tutorials and seminars. Lectures are an important part of the structure of college study and missing them means you will miss out on useful information that could help your performance in tutorials, seminars, essays and exams. It may be easy to skip lectures, since the lecturer rarely records attendance or absence, but, in both the short term and the long term, you will miss out on crucial learning.

However, some lecturers are so wrapped up in their subject and specialist research that they really don't care too much about their style of presentation to first-year students, who don't share their in-depth knowledge, and they have been giving the same old lecture for years and years. If you feel you could spend your time more constructively studying in the library and if the lecture is really dull then there's no obligation to stay. Slip out quietly at a convenient point, and no one will question your departure.

If you miss out on an important lecture, through timetable clashes or illness, you should contact the lecturer and ask them if they provided any hand-outs, recommended any further reading, or if they could let you have any lecture notes. This is much more reliable than using the lecture notes taken by your course mates, who may have only managed to jot down irrelevant details and produce an interesting doodle before drifting into reveries during the most important part of the lecture.

If you are too shy to ask a question in front of everyone in the lecture theatre, or if they run out of time for further questions, you can approach the lecturer at the end. If they haven't time to stay and answer your questions then they will probably be able to fit you in at some later date or point you in the direction of some further reading.

Most lectures are repeated each year and you may find that lectures you miss in your first year can be seen again in the second year. But don't rely on this being the case. Course syllabuses often change and a particular topic may be dropped from the course or a particular lecturer or expert in the field may move to teach abroad. Also the lectures aimed at first-years will be catering for the gaps in their knowledge, as a foundation course in the subject, and so might be quite irrelevant for second-years who have been working intensively in the subject for over a year. It might be tempting to try to fool yourself that you can catch up on this year's work next year, but in most cases the work load increases year on year and you will probably find it impossible to fit into your schedule.

Seminars

Seminars are held with groups of around ten to twenty students and are often based on a theme or topic of a course option and will cover the term or semester with one or two seminars each week. The same seminar tutor will lead each seminar, but the format is much more informal than a lecture and is centred around group discussions. Because so much time is spent on discussion it's difficult to take comprehensive notes, and you will probably find that you will make more notes during independent study and through reading the books on the accompanying reading list. Usually each student will be required to present a paper to the seminar at some point through the term and these topics are usually allocated in the first week. The prospect of leading a discussion in front of a group of people you don't really know can be daunting, to say the least, but everyone gets nervous and it is much easier than you think once you get started.

A seminar paper is basically an essay which you present to the seminar group, and is best written in note form rather than as an essay as it makes it much easier for you to read and is much easier to listen to. Back up your points and liven up your presentation with visual aids and hand-outs, and be sure to speak slowly enough for everyone to follow your line of thought and to jot down notes. If you run into trouble, your seminar tutor will discreetly enter the discussion and prompt and encourage you and the other students, so don't worry too much about floundering.

You can expect to have to produce at least two pieces of written work in the form of essays or reports on subjects covered in the seminar, and seminar courses usually make for the basis of exams to be taken at the end of the semester or as part of your final exams.

Tips on Seminars

Seminars are intensive study sessions and the knowledge you pick up will almost certainly form part of your exams or assessment towards your final grade, so make sure you do lots of preparatory reading and follow-up work to make the most of it.

Encourage others in your group by listening carefully and with interest to their presentations and asking questions. Hopefully they will do the same with you. This also helps loosen up the tension, especially with first-time nerves.

If you miss a seminar because of illness, you should ask around for copies of other people's notes, copies of any hand-outs and a copy of the presentation made by your fellow students that day.

If you are ill (not just nervous) and can't make your own presentation, you should call into the college and let your seminar tutor know as soon as possible so they can prepare an alternative presentation in your absence.

Keep in touch with class-mates in your seminar group and swap essays and notes. If possible try to tackle different topics so that, come exam time, you all have the benefit of sharing extensive research on every topic covered throughout the seminar course.

Using the Library

Most students eventually end up spending a great deal of time in the college library. This is a vast resource centre, stocking books, periodicals, newspapers and magazines, audio-visual materials such as film and video, old exam papers, academic texts and research produced by academics from your college and others. Some books are available for loan, some for short periods of time, such as overnight loan only, and some for longer, and some are for reference only. The library also provides study space for students who wish to stay and study in the library. There will also be photocopying services or a coin-operated photocopier for you to use.

Libraries usually run induction courses at the start of term and it will be well worth your while spending some time being shown around and taught how to use the elaborate computerized reference systems now installed in most college libraries. You will also need to gen up on the rules of borrowing, the rate of fines, and the opening times in order to make the most of the huge resources on offer.

Don't be afraid to ask for help. College libraries are usually huge and confusing and the college librarians will be keen to help out if you have any problems tracking down the materials you require.

Essays, Reports and Dissertations

The trials and tribulations of essay deadlines exasperate even the most conscientious students. Like all deadlines, they just sneak up on you. The key is to start working, taking notes and forming an outline of your essay as soon as possible. Track down the necessary reading materials, books and periodicals long before the essay is due. It goes without saying that if you have only a few days you can be fairly certain the book you need will be out of stock in the library and the periodicals you need will be on loan elsewhere. Preparation is the only solution. Leave yourself plenty of time to proofread and make revisions and corrections.

Essays for college have to be written in a very particular way and you should check with your tutor as to the exact etiquette for your course work. You would usually expect to include a bibliography, including the date and publisher of any books you use, and the origin of any articles you may have quoted from and to source and date every quote and reference. You may find that your tutor is particular about the size of margins, double-spacing and the use of italics, so check it out with them before you start. You should always be careful to write to the length set. Writing reams of extra pages can be just as bad as handing in a few paragraphs. Your tutors or assessors will want to see that you are learning to develop arguments within a set formula, and pages of extra ramblings and unnecessary background won't win you any prizes.

Don't worry about being a perfectionist. Do the best you can. You will be learning all the time and perfecting the skills of essay writing as you go along. Eventually you will realize that you can only do so much in the time set. The best-written essays are produced when students are both informed and relaxed enough to write fluidly.

Most colleges expect students to produce typed copy these days and you might find your handwritten scrawl is not acceptable. In colleges where they insist on typed scripts they will provide computer terminals and access to word processing for all students, so don't worry too much about having to shell out for the latest in digital technology.

If you get really behind because of sickness or another reasonable problem and you feel you won't be able to make your essay deadline, you should start negotiating with your tutor over an extension to the deadline date as soon as possible and certainly well before the day it has to be in. Most tutors are sympathetic, especially if you have been ill or have lots of deadlines coinciding in one week.

Studying on Your Own

Some students prefer to work in the peace and quiet of the library. Others prefer to study in the comfort of their own home. There are up sides and down sides to both options and it might take a while to work out which suits you best. The important point is to make sure you are organized and can't be easily distracted. Studying at home might be easier for you but it might be difficult to drag yourself away from the TV or from flatmates, friends and phone calls. You also stand more of a chance of being interrupted. Studying in the library means you are limited to the library opening times (although most college libraries open late and at the weekends) and to the space available there and it's not so easy to nip off for a cup of coffee and a proper rest.

Tips on Studying

Most people find they can study intensively only for around forty minutes and then need to take a break. After a short time you will find the formula that works best for you, but you will probably find that you absorb more in short intensive sessions than in hours and hours of reading.

Cramming is never a good idea and you usually end up wasting more time than if you spent that time trying to study properly.

Set yourself a target for each session of study, to read to the end of the chapter or to complete two pages of notes, for example, and then reward yourself with a break.

Sometimes it helps if you work in partnership with others and set yourselves targets and reward yourselves with set breaks. Many students find that working in the library and then meeting at the end of an hour for a chat and a coffee is the most productive way to study. It gives you something to look forward to and someone with whom you can chat over some of the subjects you have been studying.

Draw up a timetable of your deadlines for the term and for each week and make sure you allocate enough time for everything. It helps to draw up a list of what you have to do, what you ought to do, and what you would like to get done each week. Set yourself targets and revise the list as you go along. Inevitably you'll run out of time for some of the targets and these will have to slip on to next week's list.

Revision

When exam time comes along, make sure you have plenty of time allocated for revision and that all your notes are up to date and organized. Revision is all about condensing your knowledge into memorable chunks that can be regurgitated and developed during the exams and is certainly not about learning new topics for the first time. Stick to the work you have done and condense your notes into bite-sized pieces.

It always helps if you can revise with a friend and this certainly relieves the monotony of re-reading your old notes. Make sure you get hold of old exam papers and practise answering the questions in the time set. Your tutor might be able to arrange for a mock exam for you if you feel really nervous of coping with college exams or you could stage a mock exam with your friends and time yourselves to answer the questions of an old exam paper. Your tutor will be happy to look over your answers and give you some guidance on where you are going wrong or right.

Failing Your Exams and What to Do If Things Go Wrong

If you do fail an exam – and it is not unusual – you can usually appeal or resit the exam at a later date. The important thing is to get advice from your course tutor as soon as possible, as exam regulations vary from college to college. It may be that your course work will be enough to get you through the requirements for the course or that a fail mark in just one module won't necessarily mean the end of your college career. There may also be other circumstances that you have not necessarily been aware of, such as problems with the course organization. Ask your student union for help. If you feel you put in a good performance and have been marked unfairly, you can ask your student union or your college tutor for advice on appealing against your grade, especially if your course work has been up to scratch.

If you have any medical certificate or possible problem that could explain your performance, you should make that known as soon as possible, preferably before the results are published.

If you do decide to leave the course altogether, your local education authority will ask you to pay back your grant, but only from the date that you leave. If you have to resit next year, your local education authority will not normally pay for your fees or your grant for that extra year, but you may be able to take just the exam without attending college for a whole extra year.

Changing Course and Changing College

Sometimes things just don't work out the way we thought they would, and some students, especially in the early part of their course, find that the course or the college isn't really what they expected or what they want right now. Changing course can be relatively easy if there are spaces available on the course you want and your own college department is happy to let you change.

Changing college can be harder since different colleges have different entrance requirements, and you will need to obtain two letters of approval for the transfer and have a firm offer of a place before your local education authority will agree to pay for the transfer. It is best to make enquiries as soon as possible, as it is usually difficult to transfer colleges beyond the end of the first term of your first year without losing your eligibility for a grant and for fees to be paid. If you leave within the first term and a half, your local education authority will treat this as an error of judgement on your choice of college and it will not affect your eligibility for a grant for a new course at a new college next year.

The important thing is to get advice as early as possible. Talk through your problem with your tutor or a welfare adviser from the student union, and you will find their advice will be objective and fair. You will have to act quickly if you want to ensure you escape the complicated rules about eligibility for fees and grants and they will be able to give you help on how they may affect your particular case.

Problems with Your Course and How to Complain

If you have a complaint about the course or about the college, the first place to go is the student union. Student unions were set up to provide students with representation to the college, to defend students' rights and to negotiate on behalf of students when problems arise. If you have any problems with your course then pop along to your student union for advice where student-elected officers who have been specially trained to deal with students' complaints and represent their views to the college will be able to advise you on the next possible course of action, and will negotiate on your behalf. Most colleges also run course-representative schemes, with students from each year in each department elected to represent the views of the students on that course to the department authorities and, through the Student Representative Council and the student union, to the college authorities.

Student unions and the National Union of Students set up the NUS Student Charter several years ago, which lists students' rights to basic principles like good teaching, clear outlines of the requirements of your course, and access to resources like libraries and computer centres, as well as rights for nursery provision, access for students with disabilities and the right to representation, and colleges have pledged to provide students with the highest standards of teaching, access and resources possible. But, of course, from time to time things do go wrong.

If you feel your course or your college is letting you down and hindering your chances of succeeding academically, you should raise the matter with your course representative or with your student union. You could even get elected yourself and represent the views of other students to the college community.

Chapter 4 / **Living**

Never mind overdrafts and exams, your greatest worry and your biggest single expense will always be accommodation, unless, of course, you happen to live at home or have fabulously generous parents who buy you your own place.

For new students there are several options for accommodation. Most new students go into halls of residence or college accommodation, and most universities and colleges try to make sure there are enough places for all new students who want them. Alternatively you could go into private rented accommodation, which could be anything from a room in a shared house, a bedsit or a flat to a converted barn if you get lucky. Second-year students are usually expected to take privately rented accommodation and often end up sharing a house with friends. Final-year students have the option of taking a limited number of places in halls or staying out in privately rented accommodation.

Halls of Residence

Halls of residence are a unique feature of student life. They vary in size and standard but all come with small box bedrooms kitted out with regulation student furniture. Walls are whitewashed or painted a fetching shade of beige, carpets are wiry, stiff and brown, and the curtains are always dirty and usually in a fabric which best suited the 70s but is here till the millennium. The furniture itself will be a narrow single bed, a small bedside table, a desk, a chest of drawers, a very narrow wardrobe, a comfortable chair and a desk chair. The walls will be lined with two or three shelves. If you are lucky and the hall is especially modern, you may find you get an *en suite* bathroom, but usually bath, showers and toilets are shared and situated down the corridor.

Other shared facilities will usually include a TV room, launderette or at least a broken-down washing machine, pay phones, kitchens or dining halls and possibly a games room. The halls will provide you with sheets and pillowcases and possibly a duvet and blankets, and most operate a laundry service for clean sheets each week.

Hall fees are paid termly and by cheque within the first two weeks of the start of each term. If you decide you want to leave you will normally be required to stay until the end of term. Hall fees can be expensive, depending on the halls you end up in. Universities have upgraded a lot of halls recently to attract conference trade through the summer vacation and the swisher halls will cost a good deal more than the shabby ones.

Halls are governed by the hall wardens, who will also live in the hall. They can be academic staff from the university who take on this additional responsibility or they may be full-time administrators, depending on the size of the hall. Their job is to ensure the smooth running of the hall and to keep some form of law and order. Most halls also operate a senior student scheme with a responsible student, usually a final-year student or a postgraduate, who is on hand to help students with problems and assist the hall warden. In the true tradition of student democracy, each hall will have its own committee, with elected or nominated students meeting with the warden to arrange social activities and discuss any problems or suggest improvements. Usually the only time all the students of a hall get together is when someone sets the fire alarm off in the middle of the night, but many halls do provide social events and some halls even have their own bars.

Halls are either catered or self-catering. Catered halls are more expensive because they provide meals, usually breakfast and an evening meal. If you have a phobia about cooking and don't trust yourself to be able to balance both your diet and your bank account then catered halls may be the best option. Self-catering halls offer shared kitchens – usually shared by about ten students.

Each kitchen has a huge fridge, a dilapidated cooker, a sink, an industrial-size toaster, microwave, cupboard space and lockers, and a huge table surrounded by highly uncomfortable, plastic moulded chairs. Although the hall will employ cleaners to keep the entire place spick and span, you will be expected to keep the kitchen in a reasonable state, and to do your own washing up. Fines are imposed on all the members of a kitchen that fails an inspection by the hall warden.

Rules and regulations about halls do vary from hall to hall and college to college, but there are some set and standard rules that always apply. Among the fire safety rules, there's no cooking in your bedroom (just in case you were tempted to plug in the deep-fat fryer and rustle up some chips in the luxury of your own room), no setting off fire alarms just for fun (an expellable offence), or tampering with the fire extinguishers or propping open fire doors. Overnight guests are allowed but must be signed in (in case of a fire), hall fees must be paid on time, posters must be put up with Blu-Tack and nothing else, and your room and shared kitchen must be kept clean, and will be inspected from time to time. Fines are often imposed on those who break the hall rules, but for serious offences like setting off fire alarms you could find yourself expelled and barred for life from taking a place in halls. The one rule which is always broken is no noise after 11 p.m., but most students will complain if they have a particularly noisy neighbour who is disturbing their sleep and study time, especially during the exam season.

Halls are a great place to live for new students. Centrally heated, safe and secure, they provide new students with plenty of opportunity to meet people and at the same time eliminate many of the stresses and worries of privately rented accommodation or living on your own. There's always someone on hand to talk to and if anything breaks, leaks or floods there's someone on hand to fix it. The halls are usually situated on campus or close to it, meaning a saving on bus tickets and travel passes, and a few extra minutes' lie-in for the lazier student with an early lecture. There are enough people living in the hall for you to find at least someone you get on with and usually the occupants of a hall remain friends for the rest of their college life and often hall-mates become house-mates or flatmates in their second year.

On the down side, halls can be noisy, sometimes unbearably so. For some reason, male freshers seem to delight in a predilection for water fights in the middle of the night and this can be annoying after the fourth night in a row of howling laughter, heavy footsteps and saucepans of water flying through the midnight air. Rest assured that at least twice a term the fire alarm will have you standing on the front steps in your nightdress after someone accidentally sets off the fire alarm with their burning toast, and at least once a term someone will leave the bath running in the bathroom above your room and floods will seep through your ceiling and menace the electrics of your CD player. But these are all minus points that can be overlooked and overcome. Halls are a good part of student life and the best option for nearly all new students. They are also a relatively stress-free living option for final-year students, with the advantage of privacy and proximity to the library, lecture halls and exam halls – all the things other students avoid. Final-year students might grow impatient at midnight water fights and dawn fire drills, but halls provide security without the hassle of landlords and broken-down central heating.

You will be expected to apply for a place in halls in spring, and new students will make their application at the same time as they apply for a place at college. A number of places will be reserved for students coming up to college through clearing, and there will still be a limited number of places available at the start of term. If you have not found anywhere to live in the first week of term you can put your name down on the waiting list and stand a good chance of getting a place.

Some colleges provide single-unit accommodation for mature students and students with families, which are usually flats within a block very similar to a hall of residence but ensure some privacy and your own kitchen and relaxation space. Nearly all universities and colleges provide hall accommodation suitable for students with disabilities but any prospective students with a disability should enquire as early as possible as to the availability of such accommodation when they are making their application to college.

Privately Rented Accommodation

A few students take up the option of lodging with a family or with a household. In this case the accommodation is usually of a fair standard as the householder will be living there as well. Often the householder will be simply renting out a spare bedroom, possibly vacated by a son or daughter who has gone off to university in another town. There may be the option of joining the family for evening meals and you will probably be expected to contribute a set amount towards the bills in an amount inclusive of the rent. Lodging is a cheap and relatively safe housing option, if you get on with the family and they enjoy your company, but going into lodgings narrows the possibility for reckless student living, wild parties and late nights. On the plus side, this leaves plenty of time and space for quiet study.

Bedsits are usually converted houses with badly furnished rooms with a hob and possibly a microwave and fridge thrown in and a shared bathroom, but no other communal space. Bills are paid individually, and rent is usually paid monthly or weekly and in advance. The landlord may live in the house, but probably with his own bathroom and kitchen.

Many students take a shared house and rent with a group of friends, or rent a room in a house shared by strangers. Within a shared house you will usually find it furnished with the minimum of furniture and of the shoddiest standard. A badly decorated kitchen with cooker, fridge and, if you are lucky, a washing machine, a living room with a reconditioned television and out-of-condition sofas, and a bathroom with mouldy shower curtain and a broken window are what you might expect from the communal areas of a shared house. Bedrooms inevitably vary in size from huge master bedrooms with mirrored wardrobes to tiny box rooms. Furniture might include a bed with a badly stained mattress and, in some cases, a wardrobe, desk and chest of drawers. You may find, however, that you have to invest in your own desk and bring some furniture from home if you intend to use your room as a study and need the comfort of a proper desk or table to write your essays. Most shared houses available for rent to students have already been home to generations of slobby students and have the scars and stains to prove just that. Gardens, if they exist, will be overgrown and litter-strewn. Student houses can be fun but they can be hell. Rent is usually paid monthly and in advance, and you will probably be required to pay a whole month's rent as a deposit, which will be refunded later.

House-hunting

Finding privately rented accommodation is an ordeal. It is often a long and arduous task, requiring stamina, persistence and determination. Expect the worst and hope for the best, and be prepared to spend a great deal of time trekking around town looking at some totally unsuitable properties before you settle for the one half-decent room you can find.

Don't expect miracles. It could take up to a week to find something safe, secure and within your price range and travelling distance to college. Invest in a map of the town and a Phonecard. You will also need your cheque book, and references. References serve to prove your existence and to verify that you are a reasonable and decent person who is unlikely to ruin the property. Your college tutor and a family friend are probably the best sources for references, or a previous landlord. References are simply a typed sheet addressed 'To whom it may concern' and run along the lines of how long they have known you and how they find you a responsible and reasonable person. You will need enough money to pay for a month's rent in advance and a deposit, usually the equivalent of a month's rent, so ensure you have either arranged an overdraft or have enough in your bank account to cover such a huge expense. Never carry cash around and don't hand over any cheques until you have signed the contract.

If you are looking for a shared house with friends, it is probably best to take as many of them along as is possible to save time and rows later on when you sign up for a house your house-mates hate. Never go house-hunting on your own. Take along a friend for company. It can be dangerous travelling on your own to empty properties to be shown round by strangers. It is also nice to get a second opinion.

The best places to start looking are your college accommodation office and student union notice-boards. Your college accommodation office should be able to provide you with a list of recommended landlords in the area who have been tried and tested by students in the past. They may also be able to recommend letting agencies. Always try recommended landlords and agencies first and so minimize the risk of ending up with a really villainous landlord. Usually the college accommodation office will also provide a notice-board for students to advertise spare rooms available in shared houses and for private landlords to advertise their vacant properties. This is often a good source for single rooms and bedsits.

Local newspapers and advertising sheets usually carry classified advertisements for properties to rent and it is worth finding out what days these carry accommodation adverts and keeping a careful eye out for bargains. The window notice-boards in newsagents also carry adverts and notices for rooms to rent.

Word of mouth is the best way to find the perfect home. Graduating students and second-years moving back into hall may be able to pass on their dream home to you once they move on. Asking around students and friends in years above is the best way to find a flat, house or room without all the hassle and heartache of the lottery of calling on landlords and letting agents.

Letting agencies or accommodation agencies exist in proliferation in most university towns and cities, and thrive on finding desperate students over-priced accommodation. They make their money by charging the landlord a percentage of the rent you pay so it is in their interest to promote the highest rents and they are unlikely to negotiate over the rent on your behalf. They work basically as go-betweens with landlords and tenants. They match suitable tenants with suitable properties, check out references and arrange contracts. The usual procedure is for prospective tenants to visit the letting agency (or any number of letting agencies if you want to cover as many options as possible) and to give them their details and an idea of what they are looking for: for example, how many bedrooms, what part of town and what sort of price range.

The letting agency will then either show you round suitable properties currently available or call up and make an appointment with you to visit the property and meet the landlord. If you then decide to take the property the agency will draw up contracts, check your references and take any payment for deposits and rent in advance. Some unscrupulous letting agencies try to charge students a registration fee when they first turn up at the agency. This is actually illegal. They should not charge you anything until they have found you a suitable property and you have agreed to take it. Then it is quite common for the agency to charge a fee for drawing up a contract, which can be up to as much as two weeks' rent per person. Check out any possible charges as soon as you first make contact with a letting agency and, if necessary, shop around for a cheaper agency.

When calling up about a potential dream home, it is best to ask as many questions as possible before you set off on a trip across town to meet the landlord. Double check on the advertised rent, the exact location and the number of rooms, as these fairly major details can strangely change by the time you arrive.

What to Look for

Once you have decided on your exact needs, you can start on your research. Before signing up for any potential home you will need to conduct a fairly microscopic survey of the place and the area to make sure you are going to be as safe and happy as possible. If there are problems you find while you are looking around a house, you will be in a position to ask the landlord to have these rectified before you move in. The chances of you getting your own way and ensuring your accommodation is habitable are much higher before you hand over your rent cheque than after.

Visit the area by day and by night and check out transport available to college and to the local shops. Make sure there's sufficient public transport to get you home from an evening out as well as to and from college during the day. Have a good look round the neighbourhood and work out how long it will take you to travel into college each day. You probably won't want to spend more than half an hour travelling into college and you should give the route a test run to see exactly how easily you will be able to get to lectures when you've overslept.

If you can, try and meet the current tenants and ask them about the landlord, the area and any problems they may have with the house. They will be able to give you the most honest perspective on the property, its pitfalls and problems, and on the attitude of the landlord. They may also be able to show you past bills for electricity and gas to give you some idea of the running costs of the house.

Carefully check all over the house for signs of damp, mice, ants and cockroaches and other unpleasant extras that did not make it into the advertisement. Cockroaches like warm places, so check behind the fridge and around the oven. Mice tend to enjoy kitchens, and will leave their droppings on work surfaces and inside food cupboards. A particularly revolting addition to some very damp bathrooms are slugs and other slimy creepy-crawlies, so cast a careful eye over the bathroom floor, ceiling and walls. These extra house-mates may not bother you at all but if you spot them before you move in, you can at least demand of the landlord to take urgent action to have them removed before you arrive.

Check over the heating, plumbing and electrics. Turn on the taps and check the hot-water supply. Try out the shower head and flush the toilet to satisfy yourself that these fairly basic requirements are in working order. If you can, check that radiators and heaters are also in working order. If the heating, cooker, boiler or water heater is gas, you must ask to see a certificate issued by a registered engineer with the Council of Registered Gas Installers that they have been serviced in the last twelve months. This is absolutely essential. Carbon monoxide, a silent, odourless gas, has killed over ten students in recent years and kills around thirty people every year. If they cannot provide a certificate you must insist an engineer calls and carries out the maintenance before you move in. It really isn't worth the risk. Carbon monoxide kills while you sleep. Symptoms of carbon monoxide poisoning are headaches, nausea, aching limbs and flu-like symptoms, but most deaths are sudden and unexpected. Don't be fobbed off by the landlord with stories of how the equipment is relatively new, or how they have had no complaints. They are legally obliged to carry out the maintenance work and a Council of Registered Gas Installers engineer will simply disconnect any equipment they find puts you at even the slightest risk. A particularly worrying sign of possibly lethal equipment is the flame in the boiler. If this is burning yellow rather than blue it will be highly dangerous. Check that all the flues and ventilation around boilers and heaters are kept clear and never, ever, try to block them yourself, even if there's a gale blowing and you are freezing to death. The problem is so serious that the government's Health and Safety Executive have taken action to protect students and raise awareness after a concerted campaign by the families of victims and the National Union of Students. They have set up a special freephone hotline for anyone who needs advice and you should call the Gas Safety Action Line on 0800 300 363 if you have any concerns over the safety of any gas appliances.

Check over the doors and windows carefully, especially at the locks. Look out for signs of previous break-ins on the front door. Check that all the windows open and close properly, and look out for cracked panes of glass. Check that as well as providing you with security and keeping other people out, doors and windows will be safe and will let you out in a hurry. Mortise-locked front doors and windows with bars might seem safe but in the event of a fire you will need to make a hasty exit. Many student houses, flats and bedsits are in badly converted buildings and defy all the laws about fire safety.

You will need to be able to visualize the house or room in winter as well as summer. Beautiful bay windows may be a touch nippy when the snow sets in, and check each room has a radiator or heater, and that windows and doors are properly insulated. This can save you a fortune on heating bills.

If there's anything awry, amiss or absent from an otherwise worthy potential home you can take the opportunity to get this sorted out before you sign the contract. Check on the fridge and the cooker, on the sofa and the washing machine. If the fridge is going mouldy on the inside, if the washing machine doesn't actually exist, if the paintwork is revolting and the sofa harbours fleas, you can demand action before you move in. Most students also take this as the green light to ask for more, and rightly so. You will be spending a great deal of time and money renting the place and the landlord will be making plenty out of you, so he can afford to update, fix and mend the fixtures, fittings and decoration and ensure the accommodation is fit for human habitation. You may not get a total renovation, but you should be able to get the gas equipment checked, a lick of paint in the bathroom, and the cockroaches removed from the kitchen at the very least.

Once you have agreed on changes and have made your mind up to take the place, you can go ahead with making the arrangements to sign the contract. Don't hand over huge cheques on the spot. It is not unheard of for villains to make an easy killing out of accepting huge cheques on properties that aren't even up for rent and then running off with the cheques. You will need to double check on everything and make sure you are clued up on your legal rights and the contract before you hand over the money.

Some students are tempted to find properties in the summer before term starts and to pay out a sum to keep the property on hold. This is known as a 'retainer' and while not illegal, it is unnecessary. By paying out a retainer you not only waste money on an empty home but you are also maximizing the chances of the landlord running off with your cash.

Contracts and Legalities

Once you have decided to take the property you will usually be required to sign a contract or tenancy agreement. If at all possible, get the contract checked out with your student union welfare office, college accommodation office, local housing advice centre or Citizen's Advice Bureau. Read through all the small print carefully and ask as many questions as you can if anything seems unclear.

You will also be required to sign an inventory, a list of everything included in the property. This document protects you as much as the landlord, and you should take care to check everything. The inventory will list all the mundane fixtures and fittings and should also record the state of repair or disrepair of all the contents of the house, for example the number of knives and forks, pots and pans, the state of the sofa, the carpets and the curtains. It should read something like: dinner plates, 4 (2 slightly chipped); curtains in bedroom (slightly torn on left side), etcetera. The inventory will be checked when you move out and if there's anything missing or damaged (beyond reasonable wear and tear of everyday living), you could find the cost of its replacement deducted from your deposit. Finding the full cost of a new sofa missing from your much-needed deposit money is not ideal, so it is important you double check on the state and number of everything before you sign the inventory.

Most contracts or tenancy agreements take the form of an Assured Tenancy or, more commonly, an Assured Shorthold Tenancy.

An Assured Tenancy is basically an agreement to pay a set amount of rent over an unlimited amount of time, but usually in excess of twelve months. However, the landlord cannot attempt to increase the rent until twelve months after you first move in or begin paying rent. Once you begin paying rent you are obliged to continue paying until your agreement lapses. You can appeal if you disagree with the amount your landlord tries to increase the rent by after the first twelve months have passed by approaching the Local Rent Assessment Committee. They will then assess whether the rent is in line with local rents, but they will include the average cost of cheap council rents as well as the higher rates charged for posh apartments, and it can be that they decide the rent is below the market average and actually entice the landlord to increase the rent further. An average rent, according to research by the National Union of Students, is currently £40 a week outside London, and approximately £50 in London.

With an Assured Tenancy, the landlord is legally obliged to provide you with a rent book to record your payments and is also obliged to carry out any repairs to the property. You can refuse entry to your landlord unless he gives you twenty-four hours' notice of a visit or inspection or if he is carrying out vital emergency repairs. Landlords can evict you from the property on only three grounds, unless stated otherwise in your contract. They can evict you with just two weeks' notice if you are more than three months in arrears with your rent payments, and they can evict you with only two months' notice if they decide they need the property back for personal use or if they have defaulted on the mortgage and the building society is repossessing the property to sell it. They may be able to evict you on the grounds of late rent payment when it is combined with obvious negligence on your part which is causing damage to either furniture or the property itself.

More often students will be offered an Assured Shorthold Tenancy, which always takes a written form and must run for a minimum of six months but to a fixed date thereafter. When the agreement approaches the expiry date the landlord can either offer another agreement or give you two months' notice to quit. Landlords can evict you from the property if you fail to pay the rent over three months. The law allows you to appeal over your rent to the Local Rent Assessment Committee but the landlord cannot increase the rent during the space of the agreement.

There are possibly two other forms of contract which you may be offered. A Licence Agreement should be avoided where possible. This simply gives you permission to be in the property and offers little legal protection if things go wrong. You can be evicted for no real reason, and the landlord can increase the rent whenever he so desires, leaving you with no grounds to appeal. Landlords can visit as often as they like and carry out repairs, renovation or redecoration whenever they want without asking your permission to enter the property. Some college accommodation offices offer this type of agreement to students by arranging for them to stay in council or local authority property which is awaiting renovation. When the time comes and the council decides to do the place up you are left with nowhere to live or, at the very least, the noise and nuisance of builders until they decide to move you out and move the council tenants in.

A company let or head lease is often offered to students who are renting a house from the college, who have arranged the let with another landlord. The college in this case will be the tenant, and the students' rights as tenants are simply to pay the rent and to leave at the end of the agreement. It is safe since your landlord is effectively the college authorities and so long as you don't default on your rent you should be guaranteed a trouble-free existence for the length of the agreement.

Moving out Early

If you do decide you want to end any sort of agreement you can usually do so, although the landlord could legally insist you continue to pay rent for the remainder of the agreement. You will normally be required to give a whole month's notice in writing. You should check all the clauses and amendments in your contract before you sign to ensure you have the right to leave with a month's notice if necessary. If you have any problems getting out of a contract or agreement you should contact your student union welfare office or college accommodation office.

If one of the people you live with decides to move out and their name is not on the tenancy agreement or contract you might find that you become liable for their rent. If you are planning to move in with friends, make sure you are all individually contracted rather than leaving one or two people with sole responsibility for the agreement. Even if you are joint tenants you can still be liable for rent for the rest of the agreement if the other joint tenants move out. If you have a row and everyone else moves out you could be left paying the rent on a four-bedroomed house for the rest of the agreement.

If one person moves out, you will usually be able to find a replacement student to fill the space and it might be a good idea for you to recruit a new house-mate rather than leaving it to the letting agency or landlord. Put up ads in shop windows, in the student union, in the student newspaper and in the college accommodation office and vet new house-mates yourselves.

Your Rights as a Tenant

If your landlord wants to evict you he must serve you with a court order. If he tries to disconnect the electricity, gas or water or change the locks and try to keep you out, you should seek legal advice immediately. You can appeal against a court order and you can bring legal proceedings against your landlord if he tries to evict you illegally. This is not the case for a tenant with a Licence Agreement, who can be evicted at any point.

One of the biggest and most common problems students face over renting accommodation (apart from finding suitable homes with reasonable rents in the first place) is getting their deposits returned. You should always keep a receipt of the deposit you pay out initially.

So long as your rent is up to date and the inventory has been signed and agreed when you first moved in, there can be no real reason why the landlord should retain the deposit. When the time comes for you to leave, you should take a few steps to protect your legal position in the likely event of the landlord withholding or delaying repayment of your deposit. Write to your landlord at least once a month before the end of your tenancy and invite him to inspect the property. Make sure the whole house is clean and tidy and pay particular attention to carpets, curtains, windows and woodwork. If there's any minor damage, chips, stains or rips, then try to remedy or repair them before the inspection. When the landlord arrives for the inspection ask him to point out any defects and ensure you remedy these problems as soon as possible. Make sure all the final bills have been paid and keep copies of all receipts of bills. When the time comes to move out, return the keys on the day, either in person or by registered post, and include a letter informing the landlord that you require your deposit to be returned to you within seven days. There should be no reason why this is not possible. If after two weeks you have not received the repayment of your deposit, you can visit or phone the local county court for a form and information on the Small Claims Court. Proceedings are relatively simple, fast and cheap and you can be represented in court by your student union. The Small Claims Court can deal with any amount of claims up to £1,000, but it may be that the threat of court proceedings prompts the landlord to hand over the money immediately.

Problems of racism, intimidation and harassment of student tenants are not widespread but do happen occasionally. In this case the law is on your side. Harassment and illegal eviction are criminal offences and landlords can be prosecuted, fined and even imprisoned if they are found guilty of such offences. The Race Relations Act of 1976 makes it illegal to discriminate against potential tenants on racial grounds, and should you experience a letting agency or landlord who does display any form of discrimination on the grounds of your race, you should inform your student union immediately for legal advice and support. You can also contact the tenants relation officer at the local council. Similarly the Sex Discrimination Act of 1976 makes it illegal for landlords to discriminate against women as possible tenants. If your landlord starts to harass you or make life difficult, you should seek advice immediately from the student union. You can take legal action and receive compensation if you can prove the landlord has interfered with your peace and comfort as a tenant. Keep a diary of any incidents and, if necessary, photographic evidence. Take signed statements from any friends or neighbours who witness any incidents. Lesbian and gay students are not, unfortunately, offered any extra protection under the law for discrimination over their housing but, if it happens, you should seek advice and support from your student union.

Whatever form of problem you encounter with a landlord or letting agent it is important that you let the student union and your college accommodation office know all about it as soon as possible. It may be that they have had previous complaints which could back up your case and it will certainly mean that they can blacklist those landlords and letting agencies who are causing students problems, and therefore protect future tenants. If no one complains, the landlord will simply carry on getting away with it, at the expense of students.

Getting into Rent Arrears

If you fall behind with your rent at any point or if any of the other tenants fails to pay, you should get advice as soon as possible. Don't try to ignore the problem. You could end up homeless and owing large amounts of back rent. Contact your student union for advice on hardship loans or grants and talk to your bank manager. Contact the landlord or letting agent and assure them you are sorting out the problem. A bounced cheque or a direct debit which has been refused will cost you dearly in terms of interest and fines from the bank and it won't help matters with your landlord. Don't wait for the problem to go away – it won't.

Things to Sort out Before You Move in

With all the pieces of legal paper signed, sealed and sorted, the cheques cashed and the receipts safely stowed away, you can begin planning to move in. But before you start stacking boxes in the boot of your parents' car and looking longingly at the latest range of goodies in the Ikea catalogue, you will need to sort out a few practicalities.

Firstly you will need to contact the gas and electricity boards and ensure supplies will be on in time for your moving-in date. Their telephone numbers are listed in the telephone directory, or you can visit the local showroom, usually on the nearest High Street, to arrange the reconnection of supplies.

Electricity

Your local electricity board will provide you with all the necessary forms to start your account, and will ask only for basic information. Depending on which option you take up for repayment you may need your bank details to set up a direct debit, and details of any electricity bills you may have had at a previous address, which will eliminate the need to pay a deposit. Most electricity boards encourage students to pay by a rechargeable key meter. The electricity board install a key meter free of charge and no deposit is required. They will provide you with a couple of small plastic 'keys' which basically slot into the meter to charge it up. The keys can be recharged at shops, off licences and in High Street electricity boards, and you can charge them up by £5 a time. The beauty of this scheme is that it eliminates the shock of a hefty bill at the end of a quarter, and is the preferred method of payment for students. The main drawbacks are that you have to remember to charge up the key and that the electricity can run out in the middle of the night and it may be difficult to find your spare charge key in the dark. But the rows you are likely to have over who has to charge up the key this time are not going to match the scale of splitting a bill of £80 at the end of the quarter.

Alternatively you can pay a deposit and arrange for bills to be paid in advance by direct debit each month. The electricity board calculates the average bill per quarter and then deducts a sufficient amount from your bank acount each month to cover the payment. This is usually around £20 a month for a house shared by four people, but will vary depending on whether you run a washing machine or have electric heaters and cookers, or other high-usage equipment. The electricity board can provide you with a booklet free of charge detailing the average consumption of household electrical equipment.

There are two basic rates of charges for electricity and you should choose the rate which suits you according to when you make most of your electricity consumption. The domestic general purpose charge is about 7p a unit with a standing charge each quarter of around £11. But if you tend to use up more electricity after midnight you may prefer to switch to Economy 7 rates. With Economy 7 you pay a higher standing charge of around £14 a quarter and the rate per unit during the day is around 7p, but after midnight and before 8 a.m. the rate per unit is reduced to just under 3p. Economy 7 is the preferred method for families who can put on the washing machine on a timer switch and save money. It might not always suit student consumers unless they have particularly nocturnal habits. VAT is added to all bills and currently stands at eight per cent.

Once you've signed all the forms and arranged a method of payment you can ask the electricity board to visit on the morning you are due to move in, to reconnect the supply, to read the meter or to install a key meter. Make sure the previous tenants have settled the bill but insist on a meter reading on the day you move just to make sure you are not later charged for any bills run up beforehand, even if the property was empty.

The electricity board will be able to carry out an inspection of the property and check all the wiring if you want and you can arrange for your landlord to pay if he agrees. This is useful especially in older buildings, but your landlord might not be so happy to have any faults highlighted which may need repairing. However, it would be to your landlord's advantage as well as yours to eliminate the chances of the place going up in smoke because of faulty wiring.

If you are being billed for electricity and fail to pay on the red bill they will threaten to disconnect the service, which will not only cause you huge problems but it will also cost a fair amount to get a reconnection. Similarly if you default on any direct debits for electricity, you could face disconnection. If you are having problems paying a bill or have overlooked a red bill and have a disconnection notice you should contact the electricity board immediately. They can arrange for a repayment scheme and will listen to your problems but, if you ignore it, they will just cut you off. If you have paid or intend to pay but have received a notice or final reminder, you should still call.

Gas

Your local gas board will encourage you to pay by direct debit, which means you won't have to pay a deposit and again saves on the shock of a giant bill landing on your doormat, and you will have to fill in a number of forms with all your bank details to apply for reconnection. You will also need to arrange for the gas board to visit on the day you move in to read the meter. The charge for gas is around 10p per day with units charged at just over 1p per unit. VAT is also added to gas bills. The gas board can also give you advice on having any gas appliances serviced before you move in. The charge can be made to the landlord who is legally required to ensure all equipment is serviced at least once a year.

As with electricity, you can find yourself facing real problems if you fail to pay a bill on the final demand or default on a direct debit. Again, contact the gas board immediately: they are usually sympathetic if you have problems paying. The important thing is to make contact and ensure the disconnection is stopped before it is too late. If you have received a final reminder or a disconnection notice and you have paid or intend to pay, you should still call to let them know.

From time to time the gas and electricity boards do make mistakes in calculating bills and if you think your bills are too high or you seem to be using a huge amount of units, contact them for advice. They can investigate and take new readings. Often bills are an estimate rather than based on an actual reading and these estimates might be based on the previous tenants' high consumption record or a local average for your property and this might not necessarily tally with your real consumption.

Telephone

Most student households can't live without a phone but this is undoubtedly one of the biggest household expenses and the source of some serious rows when it comes to splitting the bill.

Ideally you should contact British Telecom as soon as you know you are going to move in. If you can take over the line before it is disconnected you can save the £10 reconnection fee. If you are going to have a new line fitted, if the house is totally without a phone, it will set you back the best part of £120. To apply for a phone line call BT sales and ask them to send you the appropriate forms, which will simply require your signature. Deposits are at the discretion of BT and will be based on your credit record with past phone bills. If you have always paid your phone bills you should get away without a deposit. If you have never had a bill in your name before they will base their decision on your parents' bill-paying record.

The cost of renting a line is around £25 a quarter, and units are charged according to time and distance. BT can send you a booklet, *Your Guide to Telephone Charges*, detailing all the current charge rates for calling the UK and abroad and the different rates for different times of day.

You can rent a coin-box but the minimum contract is for eighteen months and therefore not suitable for most student houses, and 5p out of every 10p you spend goes towards the rental. Alternatively you could club together and buy your own coin-box phone for around £200.

There are three ways to eliminate the possibility of World War

Three breaking out when you get the phone bill. The first, and rather drastic, measure is to change the line to incoming calls only. You can still make 999 calls but otherwise all outgoing calls are barred. Your friends and family will be forced to call you on their own bill.

The second way to save arguments is to persuade your parents to agree to a BT Chargecard. The cost of all your calls made from your own phone will then be listed on their phone bill but under a separate heading so you can pay them back if they need or want you to. Application forms and information on the Chargecard scheme are available from BT on 0800 345 144.

The third and most time-consuming method of monitoring the exact splitting of your phone bill is to request a fully itemized bill, which will list every single call by number, time and date, with the exact cost. This can run to pages and pages and take days of calculation and allocation to find the true cost of each housemate's bill. It may help if all the occupants of the house record their calls in a book kept by the phone for cross-referencing against the itemized bill.

If for any reason you fail to pay a phone bill after receiving a final reminder, you will be disconnected after seven days and sent a notice informing you of an expiry date for your phone line after the next seven days. If you pay the bill before this expiry date, you will be charged around £35 for a reconnection. If you don't pay before the expiry date BT will insist you pay the full amount of nearly £120 for a new line. If you are having problems paying, you should call BT and talk about repayments, but they are not as sympathetic as the gas and electricity boards when it comes to reversing a disconnection notice, and you should call them as soon as you receive a final reminder to prevent any reconnection charges.

Some students find that the cheapest and most convenient way of keeping in touch is to invest in a cheap mobile phone. After the initial outlay and a monthly charge, the call rates can be quite cheap if you shop around for the phone network which suits your location and the distance of your calls. Some mobile phone companies offer free calls in the evening or at weekends within the confines of a certain area. Contact your local mobile phone shop for details but don't rush into signing a contract. They can be very tricky to get out of and the monthly charges might not be as cheap as they first seem. Similarly call rates out of the cheap or free zone might be well over the price of a normal BT home line call rate. Research all the financial implications before signing on any dotted line.

Council Tax

Students are exempt from Council Tax. Your college will issue you with a certificate confirming your student status specifically for the purpose of exempting you from the Council Tax. Take this certificate to your local council's Council Tax office as soon as you can to make sure you are not sent a bill by mistake. The college can offer replacement certificates if you lose the first copy but it may take some negotiation.

The one problem with the Council Tax is that the bill is strictly speaking sent to the household. If one or more of the occupants of your house are not students then a bill will be sent for the household; although students can legitimately argue they are exempt, you may find it causes some rows. Seek advice from your student union if you do find there are problems with a bill or if you are sent a bill by mistake. Defaulters on Council Tax are dealt with sharply and severely and you could find yourself facing a court summons for a bill you are not really supposed to pay, so you need to make sure the council are aware that you are a student and you have presented them with the certificate. If there's just one non-student in your household, they can apply for single-occupancy billing, which entitles a discount of twenty-five per cent on their bill.

TV Licence

You are legally obliged to have a TV licence if you have a TV. You need only one licence per household but if you are living in a hall of residence you will need your own licence for a TV in your room. Failure to hold a current TV licence can result in a big fine, and it is relatively easy for the TV licensing authorities to find out who is using a TV without a licence. Forms for TV licences are available from the post office and you can arrange payment by direct debit either quarterly or monthly. Current charges for TV licences are £86.50 for a colour set or £28.50 for black and white, but the charge is set by the government each year.

Water Rates

As tenants you should not have to pay for water, and the landlord should pick up the bill for water rates. If you are sent a bill, send it on to the landlord. If they try to make you pay, you should contact your student union for help with clarifying the situation to the landlord.

Registering to Vote

As soon as you move in you should contact the council offices for a voter registration form. At the moment all students in halls are automatically registered to vote when they take up their places, but students in privately rented accommodation will have to contact the council to get hold of the form. You have a right to vote in all the local, general and European elections and you should take the opportunity. Do this as soon as you move in to guarantee your right to vote.

Safety

Ideally your landlord should make sure your new home is safe but many landlords renting property to students don't really care about your health and safety; their interest lies in your rent cheque alone. Unfortunately you are going to have to take some steps to make sure you are safe in your own home. The law is on your side as landlords are legally obliged to cover basic safety standards, and, if you need back-up, contact your student union or call the local Environmental Health Officer, who can check up and prompt your landlord into action.

Before you move in, invest in a couple of smoke alarms. Costing less than £5 these really can save lives. Smoke alarms are so cheap and yet so essential it is almost not worth negotiating with the landlord over why they have not been provided, and they can be picked up from Woolworths, DIY stores and supermarkets. The best places to put them are in the kitchen (since most fires start there) and in the highest point of the house (as smoke rises) usually on the ceiling at the very top of the staircase or the highest point in the hall if the house is on one level. You could also buy a smoke alarm for your own room just to be sure. Test the alarm once a fortnight – by pressing the small button usually in the centre or at the side of the alarm – just to check the batteries are still in working order.

Student houses are usually badly converted, to cram in as many rooms as possible, and fire exits might not be up to the required amount. A phone call to the Environmental Health Officer or to the local fire station can help with getting action from your landlord. Student houses are notoriously dangerous and the risk of being trapped in a fire is greatly increased if there are insufficient fire safety measures, exits and smoke alarms. Don't let your landlord get away with renting out a death trap.

The safety of all gas appliances must also be checked and if you have not seen the certificate issued by an engineer registered with the Council of Registered Gas Installers to say that all appliances, including boilers, heaters and cookers, have been checked within the last twelve months, you can contact the Gas Safety Action Line on 0800 300 363 for advice on dealing with your landlord. Many landlords, renting out run-down accommodation to students desperate for somewhere cheap to live, will try to get away with old appliances which could kill if carbon monoxide starts to seep out. You can buy carbon monoxide testers from DIY shops, which will alert you to the dangers of any equipment, but you should make sure all the appliances have been serviced.

Living Together

You've got your dream house, you've got your friends, you are already planning a giant house-warming party and worrying about what to wear. But house-sharing heaven can turn into hell. If you want to stay friends and live together, it is going to take a lot of hard work and more than a few days of gritting teeth.

Moving in with other people, especially if you are already good friends, can be thrilling. Planning parties, cooking up meals together, going shopping, having nights in – it can sound like it's going to be a riot, a non-stop roller-coaster of fun. The truth is it probably will be. But at some point the riot can turn into a row. Other people can be hell, and even the best of friends can end up falling out over toilet rolls, tea bags and telephone bills when living together in close proximity.

There are no real ground rules for getting along, and despite the best intentions to have weekly meetings, to organize rotas and to respect other people's time and space, the moaning, the groaning and rowing are almost inevitable.

Here are a few tips to help prevent tears before the first term ends, as you get to grips with all the faults and foibles of your house-mates from hell.

- Forget all about rotas and rosters. They never work. Don't attempt to instil any sort of discipline over your house-mates and their share of the housework. It is amazing how quickly you discover other people's low standards. Cleaning the bath, doing the washing up, putting the Hoover round occasionally and other mundane tasks are never as high on their list of priorities as they will be on yours, but they will be thinking just the same of you. If you want the dishes washed or the bath cleaned you might as well do it yourself. Persistent offenders might respond to gentle prodding but becoming the house nag will only put you in a bad mood. Do your bit to keep yourself happy and try and live with the grime and slime of everybody else. It is probably easier to go with the flow, relax and try to ignore the build-up of dust than to work on building up tension by continuously setting tasks for your slovenly house-mates.

Sally, a third-year student at University of East Anglia, has just moved back into halls after a year sharing a house with four girls. 'We were the best of friends and had spent all the first year together but once we moved in and lived together I suddenly saw a different side to their characters when it came to keeping the place even slightly clean. Kate would leave cigarette butts in the kitchen sink; Sasha never once washed up to my knowledge; Heather's room was a pit; and as for Amanda, she would leave cups, plates and glasses everywhere – in the bathroom, behind the television, by the phone, under her bed. They would be growing mould. One day I went round and blitzed the place and no one said a word. I don't know if they even noticed. It was really starting to get to me and eventually I snapped and told them all they were slobs. That was when they accused me of never rinsing out the bath! I realized I could not win and decided it was not worth falling out over the state of the house – we were still having a good time. I would moan to myself from time to time, but I learnt to just step over the plates on the stairs, to wash up my own stuff and forget about the rest.'

- Don't try to enforce communal shopping on other people. Have a joint kitty for tea bags, coffee and toilet rolls but don't attempt to share anything more. This is a great source of gripes. 'Where's all the pasta gone? I only bought some the other day and it's all disappeared' is the main moan in student houses the length and breadth of the country.

Hazel was at Manchester University and graduated last year. 'I moved into a house with five girlfriends. Someone suggested we share food and washing powder and stuff like that. Well it worked for a week before we all started complaining about how Patty was eating all the food, cooking up meals for her boyfriend with our stuff. In the end we went back to buying our own food, like we had done in halls, and having joint meals every now and again when we'd pool our ingredients. It could not have worked any other way. And, anyway, I hate lentils and it was all they seemed to buy.'

- Have a bit of respect for other people. If someone asks how long you are going to be on the phone or in the bath, it means they want a go themselves. If you can cut short your soak or call back your friend later it will mean you can ask a returned favour when your house-mate is next monopolizing the bathroom.
- Try to arrange for bills to be paid by direct debit to eliminate huge bill-splitting sessions, when arguments about who watches more television, who cooks most often, who has too many hot baths and who gets the most use out of the washing machine or the toaster can lead to major battles. Agree to split the service bills for gas and electricity and arrange for the bills to be paid monthly rather than quarterly to reduce the shock factor. As for phone bills, this row is unavoidable unless you take the phone out altogether.
- Have as many parties as possible. Parties diffuse tension. They give you a chance to plan together, to get dressed up, worked up and excited. They break the routine of everyday living and liven up the house. Whenever things are getting down, suggest a party – even if it's just a small get together. But check it out with everyone in the house. It's no good if you plan the wildest night ever on the eve of someone else's finals in medicine, when all they want is a good night's sleep and a few quiet hours cramming and instead face twelve hours of full-on non-stop techno and guests throwing up on their bed. It is a good idea to drop the neighbours a box of chocolates and give them fair warning if you are planning a particularly noisy bash.

Natasha, a third-year at Exeter, explains, 'We had some great parties, about two a term, while I was living out of halls. It gave us something to focus on instead of the washing up and meant the house got a good clean after. We would all get together the next day and laugh at all the funny things that had happened as we all took a bin bag and picked our way through the debris of cans. It really helped clear the air and raise our spirits when things had been getting tedious.'

Chapter 5 / **Health and Happiness**

Sometime during your college life you're going to get down, you're going to get ill, and you're going to have to take responsibility for your own health and happiness. The whole way through you're going to have to take care of yourself, of your own health, safety and well-being.

Health isn't just about following a proper diet, taking regular exercise and popping a few vitamin pills. At college you get exposed to all sorts of problems you may not have had to cope with before. There are various illnesses which have a tendency to affect students which you should be wary of, like meningitis, food poisoning and depression; there are issues about sex, contraception and sexually transmitted diseases that you need to be clued up about; and there are problems like alcohol abuse, smoking and eating disorders, which can affect many students. You will also have to make sure you take proper responsibility for your own safety and your own health; and on top of the fresh vegetables and aerobic sessions we all know are good for us, you've got to make sure you have regular smear tests and breast examinations, and be adamant about safer sex.

Taking Care of Yourself

One of the most important concerns has to be taking care of your own safety. There's no need to worry yourself silly, but it does pay to be alert to danger. In recent years there has been a significant increase in attacks on women students. Campuses are vast places and even in the day time there can be danger points. You can be just as vulnerable off campus too. Precaution is the best form of prevention, and you should take care not to put yourself in danger. But first off, you should invest in an attack alarm, which can be bought at discounted prices from the student union.

If you have any concerns about your safety on campus or at home, then report the problem to the college authorities and campaign with other students for better lighting on campus, security patrols and for a women's safe transport scheme to help women travel home safely late at night. Here are the NUS's tips for women's safety, which are well worth remembering.

Getting Home

Safety in Numbers
- Arrange to meet friends or flatmates for the journey home.
- Find out if there's a women's safe transport scheme at your college – if not help set one up. Arrange a meeting time and place for groups of women in halls of residence when leaving the library, the bar, or disco or any other campus facilities at night.

Public Transport
- Stand at a busy bus stop if possible.
- Don't stand near visual obstructions if possible (near a hedge or in a doorway, for example).
- Sit near other women on a bus or train.
- Avoid empty train carriages.

Taxis
- Whenever possible, take a licensed taxi. If you have to get a minicab, always ask for identification.
- Never take a ride in an unmarked car with a driver claiming it's a minicab.
- Find out if your student union works with a women's minicab service.

Cars
- Always lock your doors when driving.
- Be careful where you park. A safe place during the day may not be so safe at night. Deserted public car parks and multi-storey car parks can be particularly dangerous.
- Be alert for suspicious characters hanging around your car as you approach.

Hitching
- Hitching is dicing with danger. Don't do it. Get a taxi.

Walking
- When walking home, try not to establish a regular pattern. Vary your route but make sure you take a safe route home.
- Be alert and look alert. Walk at a brisk pace and look back occasionally. Always look like you know where you are going. Act confident and purposeful.
- Get a personal attack alarm. Have it to hand if you are walking alone in an isolated place or late at night.
- Don't use personal stereos in isolated places or late at night. You will not be able to hear if someone approaches you.
- Walk in the opposite direction to the traffic.
- If you suspect you are being followed, go to a nearby place with people (a shop, pub or well-lit house) and ask for help.
- A set of keys, a comb or umbrella will act as a weapon if you are facing an assailant.

Entering the Home

- Be sure you have secure locks.
- Have the keys ready in your hands when you arrive home. Do not fumble for them.
- If your keys are lost or stolen, have your locks changed immediately.

- If you see anything unusual (locks or windows tampered with, for example), do not enter. The intruder could still be inside. Go to a neighbour and call the police.
- Be careful of high hedges or fences or any obstruction that could be used as a hiding place by assailants.
- If it is dark when you return home, turn on the lights as soon as you enter. Don't walk around in the dark.
- Keep your porch or hall lit at night.
- Don't leave spare keys outside in flower pots or under mats. Leave them with a trustworthy friend in case of loss.

In the Home

- Be sure you have working locks on all windows. Keep windows shut and locked if you are alone, especially if you live on a lower floor. Never sleep with your windows open.
- Keep blinds and curtains drawn after dark.
- Keep the lights on if you are leaving and returning home at night.
- Keep unused rooms and storage spaces locked. They could be used as hiding places by intruders.
- Be sure you can escape quickly in the case of an emergency. If you lock your front door from the inside, then make sure the keys are to hand.
- Don't leave out ladders, crates or anything that may be used to gain entry.
- Be very careful whom you let into the house. All too often attacks on women occur in the victims' own homes. In many cases there is no forced entry by the assailant into the home. Ask all visitors to identify themselves before you open the door.
- Ask all maintenance workers, expected or unexpected, to produce identification. Take down their details and phone their employer to verify their claim. If you are still unsure, ask them to come back at another time when you won't be alone.

On the Phone
- Do not let callers know you are alone, and don't disclose your address unless it is a legitimate query.
- If you receive nuisance calls, contact the police and the phone company immediately.
- Use only your initials and surname in the telephone directory.

Taking Action

- Help set up a women's safe transport scheme.
- Campaign or petition for better lighting at dangerous places.
- Report any defective street lighting to the council.
- Inform your hall warden or college authorities of any possible danger points that concern you.

Taking Care of Your Health

Okay, we know the story: regular exercise, healthy diet, no smoking, moderated drinking and lots of mineral water every day. Unfortunately this doesn't fit in with most student lifestyles and, since you're in charge now, there's no one to tick you off if you live off pizzas and bottled beer for a year, topped up with a liberal supply of fags and embellished with the odd run for the bus as a form of exercise. But it will catch up with you in the end. If you want to be plagued with colds and lethargy, cellulite and a bad cough, then fair enough. It doesn't take too much effort to look after yourself and you'll feel better for it. If you can fit in a bit of swimming or the odd aerobics session in between lectures and the bar, keep up your vitamin tablets, eat fresh fruit and vegetables when you can and drink a couple of glasses of water every day, then you can keep fit and healthy with the least exertion on your part.

College campuses are rife with germs and the close proximity of so many living and breathing students is a playground for all sorts of infectious illnesses. Colds and flu, food poisoning and sexually transmitted diseases spread like wildfire whenever they get the chance. Unless you love living under the duvet with a runny nose, itches in funny places and a dodgy tummy, then you're going to have to take steps to maintain your health and take care of yourself.

First of all get yourself registered with the local GP or college health clinic. Remember you can always ask to see a woman doctor if you prefer. As a new patient you should get a full MOT or a thorough health check. They'll test your blood pressure, check your height and weight and ask you for a urine sample. They can also give you advice on a healthy diet, on contraception, about Well Woman clinics – for advice on breast checks and smear tests – and answer any queries you may have about your aches, pains and day-to-day ailments, like PMT or headaches. It is well worth having this full maintenance test and booking yourself in to see the nurse at the clinic once a year or so to give you a proper going over.

Registering with a dentist might not be so easy. Many dentists now, especially in areas like London, are not keen to take on new NHS patients. If you have a need for emergency dental treatment it won't be a problem, but for regular check-ups and non-emergency dental work it's probably better to stay registered with your dentist back at home and fit in appointments when you pop back to visit your parents.

Women's Problems

The phrase 'Women's problems' might bring on a few giggles in schoolboys (of all ages) but the fact of the matter is that there are certain afflictions and illnesses which do affect women and, far from being trivial excuses to get out of games practice or as an apology on our behalf for a justifiable bad mood, these can be serious and life-threatening. Get clued up on the medical problems which do affect women and don't allow the dismissive attitude of so many men to stop you from taking possible problems seriously. Most college health centres and doctors' surgeries run weekly or monthly Well Woman clinics where you can talk to women doctors and nurses who understand these particular issues and can give you the advice, information and medical assistance you need.

- **Pre-menstrual tension** is now recognized as a medical condition and doctors have stopped telling women they're imagining things. Pre-menstrual tension can cause real problems for the women who suffer with it. Symptoms include headaches, swollen breasts, weight gain, irritability, lethargy, tearfulness and depression. Your doctor will be able to give you advice on the best course of treatment for you. You don't have to put up with suffering from pre-menstrual tension.
- **Period pain** causes misery for millions of women every month. If you suffer from bad period pain and feel that it does affect your ability to get on with your life every month, then you should consult a doctor. If you feel your doctor has not taken the problem seriously, then consult another doctor. You don't have to suffer in silence and period pain can be treated. Many women find that taking the right dosage contraceptive pill helps balance their hormones and reduce their period pains.
- **Cystitis** is a common and very irritating problem. It is basically an inflammation of the bladder and can be brought on by a number of causes. Late nights and lots of alcohol may bring on the symptoms, which include a burning pain when you pee and a feeling of needing to pee all the time. You may also experience fever and aching in your lower abdomen. You may also see blood in your pee. You can remedy the symptoms quite quickly by drinking lots of water which will help flush out your system, and by taking bicarbonate of soda hourly for three hours. If the symptoms persist or reoccur regularly, see the doctor.
- **Toxic shock syndrome (TSS)** is caused by using tampons. Symptoms vary but the onset is usually a flu-like virus, followed by diarrhoea, a high temperature, rashes on the hands and feet, double vision and hair loss. The symptoms develop very quickly

and should be treated immediately. TSS can be very dangerous and a number of students have died from it. If you do use tampons, make sure you use the right absorbency and change them regularly. Some doctors advise against using tampons at night.

- **Cervical cancer** can be prevented or treated if cancerous cells are eliminated early on. For this reason every woman should have a smear test every three years. If you haven't had one yet you should make an appointment at your local clinic or at your doctor's surgery. It is a simple enough procedure, and it doesn't really hurt. A sample of cells is gently scraped off the cervix and stuck to a slide which is then sent to a laboratory for tests. You can call or phone in for the results of the test. If the cells are pre-cancerous you will be called back for treatment to stop them in their tracks, so it is vital that every woman has a check at least every three years.
- **Breast cancer** can also be prevented or treated. Check your breasts regularly for lumps, dimples, and any changes to your nipples. If you have any cause for concern or notice anything different, tell your doctor. A lump might not necessarily be cancer at all and the chances are it won't be, but it is well worth checking it out as soon as you can.
- **Thrush** is another common affliction on campus. It can be passed through sexual contact or it can just flare up on its own from an imbalance in your acidity levels. Wearing tight clothes, especially man-made fibres, and washing with perfumed toiletries won't help matters. It can affect men as well as women, but you should look out for a thick white discharge from the vagina, itching, swelling, soreness and pain when you pee. And yes, natural yoghurt applied directly can help, as can anti-candida tablets available from health food shops or from your doctor. You might find that wearing tampons brings on an attack and it can flare up if you are taking antibiotics for another condition.

Contraception and Pregnancy

If bouncing babies aren't on the agenda for your college career, you are going to have to take steps to reduce the risk of getting pregnant, and undoubtedly you will want to protect yourself from the risk of HIV and other sexually transmitted diseases too. Most students are happy with condoms, and rightly so, since they are the only form of contraception that offers any real protection against HIV and sexually transmitted diseases. There's a never-ending supply of them on campus. You can pick them up free from the college health centre, from your student union and from the local family planning clinic and you can buy them in every college shop and from vending machines in most bars and toilets, and there's no stigma attached to having one fall out of your handbag. Most students wouldn't dream of having sex without one. However, there are always a few fools and, funnily enough, they are mostly male.

Never, ever, trust a man who says 'trust me' as a form of contraception. You can't. Whatever his excuse, whatever he pleads, it isn't true and it isn't good for you. If you can't persuade him to put on a condom then you really ought to throw him out of bed. If you are happy about dicing with the deadly dangers of HIV and a multitude of sexually transmitted diseases, but don't want to get pregnant, then you are going to have to make sure you have taken responsibility for another form of contraception.

There's no method of contraception that's one hundred per cent effective, except abstinence, and many contraceptives have side effects which might mean they are not suitable for you. Making the decision about which one suits you and your sex life is all yours, but should be based on the advice of your GP or a doctor in a family planning clinic.

The Condom

The condom is ninety-eight per cent effective if used with a spermicide. It is the number one bestseller in the student contraceptive stakes since it does offer some protection against sexually transmitted diseases. It is the only real method to fit the bill when it comes to safer sex. Men who tell you 'it feels like having a bath with your socks on' and moan about being asked politely to put one on obviously couldn't care less whether they or anyone else ends up with a nasty rash, an embarrassing itch, or worse.

The other methods of contraception available offer no protection against sexually transmitted diseases, they are all the ways whereby women have to take all the responsibility and, funnily enough, most of them have potentially dangerous side effects for the woman who's taking them.

The Pill

The pill is an oral contraceptive. If taken according to the instructions it can be ninety-nine per cent effective but, if you don't follow the instructions to the letter, it can be about as useful as eating a lettuce leaf every morning and crossing your fingers. If you miss a pill or if you're sick before it has been absorbed into your blood stream, you'll be at risk for the rest of the month, not just that particular day. The pill must be prescribed by your doctor or the doctor at the family planning clinic who should advise you on the right brand or type of pill according to your age, health and lifestyle. If you do opt for the pill then make sure you ask as many questions as you can. Cross-examine the doctor on all the potential side effects and make sure you can answer questions about the medical history of your family, especially if any of your family has suffered from thrombosis or had problems with their blood pressure. Side effects will vary according to the individual but the most common are weight gain, depression and nausea. The pill has also been linked to cancer, thrombosis and other potentially lethal illnesses. Obviously a dose of chemicals into your blood stream every day cannot be totally beneficial, particularly when this is controlling your hormone balance on a regular basis. But the most worrying side effect of the pill is that it provides no protection at all to life-threatening sexually transmitted diseases. Many men will try and persuade women that the pill is a convenient and safe form of contraception. Ask yourself exactly who it's convenient for. Could it possibly be the man, who won't worry about the side effects, won't worry about the responsibility of taking it according to the instructions to the very letter and obviously couldn't care less about safer sex? Perhaps it would be more convenient, and certainly much safer, if you kicked him out of bed.

Other Methods

- The **diaphragm** or **cap** is a rubber device inserted into the vagina before sex to cover the cervix. It has to be left in place for six hours after sex and must be used with a spermicide. It has to be fitted initially and then regularly checked by your doctor.
- The **coil** or **IUD** is, to give it the full name, an intra-uterine device. It is a plastic tubing coil that is inserted in the uterus by your doctor. It prevents the egg from settling in the uterus, so it prevents implantation of a fertilized egg rather than stopping the egg getting fertilized in the first place. The down sides are that it can cause serious damage to the uterus and affect your fertility in the future as well as causing heavy periods. It hasn't the best track record as a contraceptive and it offers no protection against sexually transmitted diseases.
- The **sponge** is basically a soft circular sponge soaked in spermicide which can be inserted into the vagina before sex and has to be left in for six hours after. It has a very high failure rate – of 25 per cent – and it has no place in the safer sex bedroom.
- **Natural methods** are definitely the worst when it comes to reducing the risk of pregnancy and do absolutely nothing to prevent the risk of sexually transmitted diseases. The rhythm method is based on working out the days in your cycle when you are least likely to fall pregnant and, given the erratic nature of student lifestyles, even the most regular girl can find her body will fall out of synch just when she thought it wouldn't, and sperm are

notoriously resilient creatures who can hang out for up to five days to hunt down an egg. Other natural methods are withdrawal, otherwise known as 'I won't come inside you', but this is very risky and even if your man keeps to his word and gets out in time there are still sperm which are emitted before ejaculation, which will be just as determined to find the egg and get into action.

After-sex Contraception

For safer-sex girls, this is what to do when the condom splits. For those who didn't bother with the safer-sex option, it's what to do when you threw caution to the wind and had unprotected sex. The morning-after pill can be taken up to seventy-two hours after sex, so it's not strictly morning-after. It is a very high dose of hormones and it can't be used as a regular method of contraception. Most doctors won't prescribe it more than three times in any twelve-month period. It won't reduce the risk of infection from sexually transmitted diseases but, if taken properly, it will reduce the risk of pregnancy. Side effects are nausea and headaches but these don't usually last for long.

What to Do if You Think You May be Pregnant

If you think there's even the slightest possibility you might be pregnant you should get a test done as soon as possible. It's not a problem you can ignore and there are some serious health risks which mean you must get medical help. The most obvious sign of possible pregnancy is a missed period, but nausea, breast tenderness and vomiting are also indications. Many women find they go off alcohol and smoking. Get a test from the local chemist's, from your family planning clinic or from the doctor's. They take merely minutes and are reliable if you follow the instructions properly. Most tests come in packets of two so you can double-check the result. If the test is positive make an appointment to see your doctor immediately.

If you decide you don't want to go through with the pregnancy, the doctor will be able to give you advice about termination. Remember it's your body and you decide what to do about it, and be very wary of anyone who tries to tell you what's best for you or for the future of the pregnancy. For impartial advice and information you can call the Pregnancy Advisory Service (local numbers will be listed in your telephone directory or are available from your student union welfare centre, college health centre or doctor). If you want to have an abortion, then the earlier the better. There is a time limit to your decision-making. You can have an abortion through the NHS or through a private clinic. NHS treatments are free but you may have to wait a few weeks for the appointment. Private clinics will charge approximately £200–£300 but the appointment can be arranged very quickly. Abortions are usually carried out between seven and twelve weeks from the date of your last period and at this stage are performed by vacuum aspiration method, which is safer than having your tonsils out and requires no overnight stay.

Whatever your plans for the pregnancy it is important that you get medical advice as soon as you possibly can.

Sexually Transmitted Diseases

There are at least twenty-five sexually transmitted diseases that could be doing the rounds in your college right now. Catchy scratchy problems that spread like mad if you're not careful. The best thing to do to avoid the likelihood of rashes, itches, warts and more serious and life-threatening infections is to practise safer sex. The symptoms of most sexually transmitted diseases are often hard to spot on a man, to the untrained eye, especially in candlelight or after a few drinks. And just because the man of your dreams looks infection-free, it doesn't mean he hasn't picked up a nasty dose along the way which he will now, unwittingly or otherwise, pass on to you.

If you've got an itch Down There, a rash, a funny discharge or experience pain during sex or when you're peeing, then check it out with your doctor as soon as you can or pop along to the genitourinary clinic at your local hospital for some tests. There are some sexually transmitted diseases which can be cleared up quickly and relatively simply with medication, there are others which could seriously affect your health and your future fertility, and there are some which could kill you. If you have any reason to suspect any sort of infection, get it seen to immediately. It might be something else or you can get it stopped before it becomes too much of a problem. And it is important you get your partners checked out too.

HIV and AIDS

Safer sex boils down to this: in the heat of that notorious delicate moment, long after you've thrown all caution to the wind, do you have the presence of mind to ask him to use a condom? Do you have the nerve to say no if he won't? Can you bring yourself to look beyond the next few hundred seconds? Or do you just go ahead and take that risk?

Media interest in HIV and AIDS has continued to wane steadily. No longer are we bombarded with health-campaign advertisements and daily tabloid sensationalism. You could be forgiven for thinking that this disease no longer represents a serious threat to the health of the nation. But you'd be wrong.

The HIV and AIDS epidemic in this country continues to grow. It is true that the majority of HIV infected individuals in this country are sexually active gay men and intravenous drug users. But the proportion of infected heterosexuals is growing steadily.

HIV is a virus which leads to the destruction of vital components in the human immune system. The body's ability to fight off infection is progressively worn down and normally harmless organisms become capable of causing severe illness. This condition is referred to as Acquired Immune Deficiency Syndrome (AIDS).

AIDS is a terminal illness. There is no cure. Currently available medical therapies amount to little more than pharmacological damage limitation. When it comes to sex the only really safe option is 100 per cent celibacy. But if, like the vast majority, you intend to continue to enjoy a healthy sex life, then make it safe. HIV is transmitted in blood, semen and vaginal fluids. Infection can be caused by the exchange of these fluids during sexual intercourse. Using a condom dramatically reduces the risk of infection with HIV and many other sexually transmitted diseases. Some ways of having sex carry a higher risk than others. Unprotected anal intercourse carries the highest risk of infection. This is closely followed by unprotected vaginal intercourse. There is also a risk of infection associated with sharing vibrators and other sex toys, again because of the exchange of bodily fluids.

Theoretically there is some risk associated with oral sex. The virus could pass from semen or vaginal fluids into the bloodstream via sores or cuts in the mouth. However, this is thought to be unlikely.

To date there have been no proven cases of the virus being passed on through kissing.

Remember that you can't tell whether or not someone is infected with HIV from the way they look or the sort of person they are. People can remain healthy for years after they have been infected with HIV. The only possible step you can take to reduce the risk while having sex is to use a condom. Always. It just doesn't make sense to take the risk.

Drugs, Fags and Alcohol

Drinking, smoking and the recreational use of drugs are often thought to be part and parcel of student life. It doesn't have to be that way. Excessive use of alcohol, and any use of tobacco and the use of most drugs is extremely damaging to your health and to your ability to get on and make the most of the opportunities to do well at college. You can hardly hope to come away with a good degree if you've spent days, weeks or months in an alcoholic blur of excess. The cost of smoking, drinking and buying drugs should be prohibitive to most students but somehow or other we find the money to indulge every now and again. The pressures to join in a non-stop party are there for you to avoid and it's up to you to make your own decisions about the risks involved in even occasional indulgence.

A wealth of literature exists warning of the dangers of taking illicit drugs. As you leaf through the catalogues of side effects and anecdotal evidence you might begin to wonder how anyone manages to take drugs while staying sane and alive. When you compare these reports to your own experiences they often don't seem quite to match up. After all, you watch your mates going out raving on an assortment of illicit substances week after week and it looks like plenty of fun. None of them seems to have gone mad yet and none of them seems to be dead. So who's telling the truth?

There are only two main myths about drugs. One is that they are going to do you harm. The other is that they do you no harm at all.

The majority of people who are part of that weekend drug culture manage to get by with no immediate overt problems. However, the more subtle effects are harder to gauge. In the absence of long-term studies of drugs, the long-term hazards are impossible to predict.

Legal or illegal, they all have their own effects, both short-term and long-term, and they carry their own potential dangers – physical, psychological and criminal. Bad things can and do happen. But as long as you are aware of the facts, you can make up your own toxin-filled mind about whether you want to take the risk. These are the facts.

All the drugs listed here may damage your health. There isn't a drug in existence which doesn't have a side effect and there is no such thing as a safe drug.

With the exception of alcohol and tobacco all the drugs listed here are illegal. This has two important implications. Firstly, there are no controls in the operation to govern their supply or use. No one can guarantee the purity or safety of illicitly acquired substances. Secondly, offences associated with possession, supply or trafficking are punishable with fines and potentially even prison sentences and you will certainly get into very big trouble with your college.

Cannabis

This is by far the most commonly encountered of the illegal drugs within the college scene. It is available as a dried leaf (grass, pot, weed), as resin (hash or hashish) or oil and can be smoked or ingested. The effects of this drug are highly variable but users most commonly experience euphoria and a sense of relaxation. Cannabis is regarded as the least dangerous of the illicit drugs. However, it is not entirely risk-free. Short-term use may induce psychosis and feelings of paranoia. Judgement, motor skills and memory may all be impaired and tasks which require skill and co-ordination, like driving or writing an essay, should not be attempted. An 'amotivational syndrome' has been associated with the long-term use of cannabis. This is a loosely defined term which encompasses a lethargic state accompanied by feelings of unease and a sense of not being fully effective – perhaps not putting you in the best frame of mind to work towards a First.

Ecstasy or E

The recent deaths and near fatalities associated with this drug have put it firmly in the media spotlight. Ecstasy is a stimulant and its use is associated with feelings of openness, trust and confidence. The milder adverse effects include depression, anxiety and disturbing hallucinations. Ecstasy is also thought to impair the mechanisms in your body which regulate heat and thirst. Deaths from hyperpyrexia (over-heating), sudden renal and liver failure have been reported. Ecstasy preparations are notorious for being highly variable in composition and purity. MDMA, the active ingredient in ecstasy pills, is often mixed with or substituted by a variety of other substances. These include speed, ketamine, LSD and scouring powder. Because of this it is impossible to assess the true risk associated with taking ecstasy even just once.

Cocaine

This drug comes as white crystals and is usually snorted, or it can be smoked or injected. And it's expensive. It produces a short-lived euphoria and induces severe psychological dependence. When the effects of the drug have worn off the user may experience depression or fatigue. The smokeable preparation, crack, is cheap and powerfully psychoactive. The hit achieved through smoking crack is equivalent to that obtained by injecting. But it is so incredibly addictive that it can lead to dependence after only the first use. Long-term use of cocaine leads to dependence and tolerance. This means that the body needs larger and larger doses to satisfy its cravings and depression is experienced if these demands aren't met.

LSD or Acid

According to a survey of fifteen- to twenty-four-year-olds in 1992, one in ten had tried LSD. Police reports suggest an upsurge in the use of the drug in the late eighties, linked to the development of the rave scene. These days it's not as popular as ecstasy but it's still there. LSD is a very powerful hallucinogen and its effects include perceptual distortion and feelings of dissociation. There is a minimal risk of physical dependence. However, users may at any stage experience a 'bad trip', provoking anxiety and panic, which in some cases can be very severe.

If someone is experiencing a bad trip, they will need looking after. Take them somewhere quiet where they feel comfortable with the surroundings. Reassure them and stay with them. The key side effect is panic, so try to calm them down. This experience should last a few hours but will be profoundly disturbing. If they become uncontrollable, hysterical or the trip lasts for more than twelve hours, get a doctor or get them to a hospital.

Amphetamines

Speed or whizz, as amphetamines are commonly known, is the most widely used illegal drug after cannabis. Speed comes as a powder or crystal and can be snorted or dabbed on a finger and placed on the tongue. It can also be smoked or injected.

Amphetamine consumption increases alertness and delays fatigue, heightening the user's ability to perform physical tasks over a long period. High doses can induce nervousness, anxiety and temporary psychosis. Use over more than a few days is limited by unpleasant symptoms, although the feeling of well-being created by the drug can lead to a period of continual use, culminating in a sudden crash into depression. Amphetamine use can also trigger underlying psychiatric problems. A psychotic state can be induced after a single use. Prolonged use is also associated with dependence and the production of a paranoid psychotic state.

Alcohol and Tobacco

Nicotine and alcohol are the most commonly enjoyed recreational drugs in society. They are legal and your student union will sell and actively promote them. They are far from harmless and, unlike the other drugs mentioned before, the short- and long-term effects are well established and documented. They are also highly addictive.

Katie recounts her experience of picking up her habit: 'I started smoking at university in my first year. Up until then I'd been a social smoker, only at weekends and only if I was drunk. At that stage I couldn't understand how anyone could possibly get addicted to these things. They smelt terrible, they tasted terrible and they usually made me feel sick. But it was a sociable thing to do. By the time I'd reached third-year finals I was getting through twenty to thirty a day.'

The bottom line with smoking is this: one in two people who smoke will die prematurely of a smoking-related disease. Smoking isn't dicing with death, it's more like playing heads or tails. Apart from the well-known risk of lung cancer, smokers may also suffer from heart disease, suppressed immunity, bronchitis, blood-vessel disease and gastric ulcers. And, of course, smoking when pregnant can adversely affect the health of your unborn child.

The psychological dependence is extremely strong. Tolerance

and physical dependence also occur. The benefits of smoking are immediate and obvious: relaxation, increased concentration, social status or just sheer pleasure. The down sides don't show themselves for years apart from the smell, the stains on your teeth and fingers, and the annoying little cough in the mornings. You may not care about the risks at the moment, but how will you feel in twenty years' time, when it's really going to count?

The good news is, if you manage to give up, most of the damaging mechanisms arrest immediately. The longer you give up for, the lower your chances of dying prematurely. If you manage to give up properly before you are thirty you can avoid most of the additional risk. After ten years' abstinence your risk of premature death from a smoking-related illness is about the same as someone who has never smoked before.

The bad news is it's bloody hard to give up. If you smoke and you want to give up there are a variety of support groups, phone lines, and helpful organizations you can contact. Hypnosis and acupuncture may also be effective. However, there is no easy answer and the key to giving up ultimately lies in your state of mind.

There are very few social events in student life that don't involve alcohol. Discount prices, endless beer promotions and all-day happy hours make it hard to resist. You'll tend to spend the whole week trying to develop a few brain cells and then Friday night killing them all off. It's a tried and tested formula and is apparently almost totally socially acceptable. For the vast majority, alcohol can be enjoyed with no ill effects. But alcohol is not harmless. Excessive use, even at an early age, can cause chronic liver disease, high blood pressure, sexual impotency, memory loss and rebound anxiety.

Each year around 500 people die because of illegal drugs while 40,000 die from alcohol-related illnesses. But still the fuss is over the dangers of E and all the other assorted mind-bending pharmaceutical products being passed around at raves and parties. Meantime, trading hands at student union bars, in pubs, clubs and drinking dives all over this land is a far more common cause of death and destruction and it's all totally legal. Around £200 million is spent each year on alcohol advertising and they still want us to buy more.

Well, naturally. Alcohol is the nation's favourite drug (forgetting all about caffeine for a minute) and students, like the rest of the population, are into it as much as possible. It makes you cool, it makes you sexy, it impresses your friends, it relaxes you and it certainly helps break the ice when it comes to approaching the partner of your dreams. And despite the murder of your grant cheque, you can pick up a pint for little over a pound and drown the sorrows of overdrafts and overdue essays with ease.

As if you needed any other inducement, much of student life is based around swigging from one bottle or another. Think of all the cheese and wine receptions at the start of term, Wednesday afternoon drinking after a bit of sport, cheap beer discos, tequila nights, cocktail nights ... virtually every ents programme reads like the diary of a hardened boozer, and however hard you try to abstain there will always be someone offering you a quick pint after the lecture or begging you to get legless at the Friday night disco. There'll be tequila-at-£1-a-shot nights, there'll be pints at £1, there'll be as much booze as you want and the bar will be open again the next day for a little hair of the dog. Getting totally blotto at least twice a term is almost a prerequisite for modern-day student living. Getting totally blotto is, as if you needed to be told, not good for you but often, despite good intentions and much like essay deadlines, it sneaks up on you and, before you know it, the room's spinning and you have a guaranteed headache for tomorrow.

Experts believe that young people (who drink more than any other section of the population) not only build up the pattern for serious drinking problems in the future during their years of novice drinking but can be seriously misled by advertising and hype.

The brewing barons have started to change the rules of the game a little. Those out-and-out hard-drink drinks are too obvious. In fashion instead are some potent combinations of pure alcohol and sugary water, packaged in a not altogether grown-up style. Cute little bottles of sweet-shop-style drinks are fast becoming a favourite tipple but the bubble-gum flavours and trendy marketing mask a potentially lethal alcoholic volume. Trendy MD 20/20 is 13.5 per cent alcohol volume, more than double the strength of Holsten Pils. The perennial student favourite, Diamond White, is 8.2 per cent, stronger than the wino's preferred Strongbow Super. And if you really want to get hammered, the cheap but not cheerful Thunderbird Red is 17.5 per cent – headache-inducing at more than three times as strong as a bottle of Budweiser. Those fancy new alcoholic lemonades and ginger beers are more potent than their friendly fizzy flavours might suggest. Getting out of it on these babies is going to cost your liver dearly, and who knows what scrapes you might end up with on the night.

Only the man on the moon can claim to know the safe limits for a lifetime of drinking. Women should stick to 14 units a week (a unit being half a pint, a small glass of wine or a single measure of spirits) and that means jut seven pints or 14 vodkas all week – and men should be wary of exceeding 21 units a week, that's just ten and a half pints a week. In terms of physical damage to mind and body, excessive use of alcohol over these limits can be more dangerous than the limited use of pure heroin, which is a pretty sobering thought, and one which you will undoubtedly recall on a particularly bad morning-after rather than on your fourteenth round the night before.

It's a popular misconception that students fritter away their huge grants on all-night binges in the student bar. All-night binges maybe, but the bars are cheap and, anyway, most of the grant cheque has already been frittered away on luxuries like rent and travel before you can think of your social life and a sensible diet. Drinking is a part of student lives and has been since the first person ever to go to university got a bit bored in between books and opened a can of lager. Keep tabs on what you knock back and remember the long-term effects of each mega-blotto session are too well known to ignore. Get out there and party, but aim to live for another day.

Here are some worrying facts about alcohol:
- Alcohol reaches the brain within five minutes of being swallowed.
- All alcohol is a depressant drug (not just gin) and slows down the activity of the brain, which means studying, exam performance and witty pithy comments to potential lovers are out of the question after half a pint.
- Eating before drinking slows down the rate at which alcohol has its effects.
- Fizzy drinks increase the speed at which alcohol is absorbed into the body.
- Alcohol affects women more quickly than it does men and the effects last longer.
- Men who drink regularly at unsafe levels risk impotency and infertility.
- It takes the liver one hour to break down one unit of alcohol.
- 18–24-year-olds are the heaviest drinkers in the population.
- There's no cure for a hangover, only prevention.

In the end, you will have to make your own decisions about which potential damaging drugs you let into your body. There's no doubt about the fact that most drugs are available within the student community and, of course, alcohol and tobacco are actively promoted.

Joy, at Reading, explains the pressures of the college scene: 'Drugs are readily available and a large proportion of students smoke dope, which is generally viewed as completely harmless. More worrying are speed and ecstasy, easy to get hold of, expensive and can be dangerous. The only drugs I use are alcohol and, less often, tobacco which, it has to be remembered, still carry risks, despite societal acceptance of them.'

Don't follow the crowd but make up your own mind about what you want to do.

Loneliness, Depression and Stress: Coping with Feeling Down

It is not unusual at all for students to feel down at some point. The problem is you can feel quite isolated and when things get too much – such as stress about exams, overdrafts, job prospects or if things just aren't living up to expectations – many students begin to question whether or not they're doing the right thing.

Miranda, at De Montfort University, was really down in her first term at university. 'I had come to university with all these expectations about the fabulous time I was going to have, but it wasn't turning out that way at all. My course was disappointingly dull, I thought Leicester was an awful city and I didn't get on very well with my house-mates. To make matters worse, every time I spoke to my school friends they all seemed to be having a brilliant time at their respective universities. What I did about it was to go and see one of the counsellors at the university. It took a lot of courage to go because I felt like a failure. As a result I decided to stick things out and to try and make the best of the situation. From then on, each year has been better than the last, so for me it was the right decision.

'I would advise any student who is down or depressed to go and see a counsellor or to talk to one of their lecturers. If things are so bad in your house, for example, that you want to move out, there are people who will be able to tell you your rights when it comes to contracts and others who will help you find somewhere new to live. Don't suffer in silence.'

As Miranda says, it takes a lot of courage and often it feels like you're giving in to defeat to go and seek help, but doing something practical and asking for advice and for support is the best thing you can do. Often the problem that's getting you down can be solved through quite practical ways and it can help sometimes just to have someone to listen. Tutors, counsellors, student union welfare advisers and hall wardens will all be happy to spare you time to talk through whatever's worrying you and will be able to help you practically.

Joy at Reading also found she got down during the first term of college life. 'Despite the large numbers of people at university, I still got quite lonely, particularly during the first year. Making friends is relatively easy but actually getting to know people so that you feel you can talk to them takes a lot longer. Continuing to make an effort to get to know people can be difficult so I kept in touch with friends from home for a bit of support. The university counselling service were also good and helped until I got a bit more settled.'

Laura, a student in London, was seriously considering giving up her course. 'I had a part-time job in the pub, I was really broke and I needed to work just to pay the rent. I'd fallen behind with my college work and failed to hand in several essays. Then I got a letter calling me in to see the Dean. I was petrified I was going to get thrown off the course. I was very worried about the bank, who were sending me demanding letters, and I couldn't sleep because of worry. I tried to bury my head in the sand for a while but finally the day arrived when I had to go and see the Dean. I was very scared and almost decided not to go at all. In the end I went to see my tutor first and just opened up to him about my money problems, and how my job in the pub was keeping me from college work, and how fed up I was. He contacted the Dean and sorted me out there. He called the bank and arranged a meeting for me to go and sort out a new overdraft limit, and he contacted my other tutors and lecturers and arranged new deadlines for my work and explained my problems to them. I had got into such a state about everything but it was possible to sort everything out. I just needed some help, some advice and some sympathy. I would recommend anyone who gets into similar worries to get help and to let the college know what's going on. They are surprisingly sympathetic and didn't treat me like the failure I thought I'd become.'

As well as tutors, student counsellors and student union welfare officers, most colleges and universities offer a night-line service run by student volunteers during term time as a confidential listening and information service. They are not there to judge you or come up with instant solutions but to listen.

Jo, at Glamorgan University, found the university counselling service an invaluable source of support when her mum died during her second year, and she says she is forever indebted to her lecturers, course-mates, flatmates and boyfriend who gave her support when she needed it most. 'I would recommend to anyone who is depressed: talk to your university's counselling service, make sure your lecturers know what's going on and lean on your friends a bit. If they're good friends they'll want to support you, even if they're a bit confused how to. Don't worry about your work too much, understand that you're not going to do brilliantly if you don't work well under pressure. Just concentrate on passing and realize that you're going to have to work hard the next year.'

It is not difficult to feel lonely at college, despite the big numbers of other people. Sometimes you might feel isolated or alone, an anonymous face in the crowd. But at least at college it is easier to get out and meet new people without appearing to be a desperate no-hoper. Join up with clubs and societies which take your fancy, get involved in student activities and get motivated with your studies, but try not to study too much on your own. Team up with class-mates or others on your course to study in the library or to discuss your subject over a few coffees. It won't take long to meet new people and it won't take too much effort. Worrying about it and hiding yourself away won't help at all. Take up the advice of others, and talk to tutors, counsellors and welfare advisers, who are used to advising students on the subject every day.

Chapter 6 / **Sex and Relationships**

When you're going off to college you'll probably take with you one or two romantic ideas. Usually these take the form of 'I will definitely be faithful to my partner from home. I'm really going to miss them, but it's going to work out', or 'I am going to meet some gorgeous people at college, fall in love, have romantic walks, candlelit dinners, leave college, get married and live happily ever after.' Sadly things are rarely that straightforward and story-book romances tend to stay in the story books. One thing is for sure, there will be lots of highs and lots of lows and nothing will stay the same in the course of your college love-life.

Then there's the business of sex. Some people do it, some people don't. Some people have been doing it for ages, others have yet to have a go. There's an awful lot of nerves and hormones, intermingled with homesickness and heartache surging through campus at the start of term. Peer pressure, temptation, confusion and intoxication might mean you end up doing something you really didn't mean to and might regret later. Whatever you get up to is up to you – so long as you are safe and your partner is willing – but there are bound to be some problems somewhere along the line.

There's no right or wrong way of doing things, and it would be silly to try and predict what will happen. Things are going to go wrong at some times and be blissful at others. The most important thing is that you do what you want, without forcing others to do something they don't want to do, and that you play safe at all times.

With relationships, we are all on a steep learning curve throughout our lives, and though you might get a lot of experience in heartaches and highlights while you're at college and it might seem like the end of the world or the beginning of the greatest romance, it is never as dramatic as all that in the cold light of day.

Relationships at college are very tricky things. It might not seem like it at first, but college is a very small place, and the people you meet will be around for a long time. It is easy to make mistakes and not be able to get away from them. You have to remember that this is just the beginning, and one failed relationship (or even ten) doesn't mean you're doomed never to find real love for the rest of your life.

Here are some popular misconceptions and truths about college romance:

- **Everyone's at it.** This is a big misconception. College life isn't as promiscuous as the tabloids like to make out. Don't feel obliged to rush out and look for love or sex. Relax and enjoy yourself. You don't have to be in a relationship to be happy – nor do you have to be in and out of everybody's beds for your entire college career.
- **Fuck a Fresher is a popular game for second- and third-year students.** Unfortunately this is true for a tiny minority of men who feel they can prey on the new intake of students who haven't been subjected to their boring chat-up lines as yet and have no idea of their appalling reputations or knowledge of their sexually transmitted diseases. Be warned.
- **If you spend your time looking desperately for love, you probably won't find it.** Absolutely true. Relax and let things happen. There really is no hurry, and if you rush about looking desperate it will send the wrong vibes out to everyone.
- **Relationships from home rarely last.** Unfortunately this is true and it might well be that your lasting love for your boyfriend back home falls at the first-term hurdle, as most do.
- **Sleeping with lecturers will improve your marks.** This is almost certainly unlikely. Affairs with lecturers are uncommon and not advised. It can get very complicated. Lecturers are supposed to declare any relationship with a student to senior staff in the department to ensure there's no favouritism or persecution,

because if things go wrong you could end up in a proper mess and with worse marks than ever.
- **If you meet someone in the first weeks, you'll be with them for the rest of the course.** Possibly, but not necessarily. You and your partner are likely to change and develop in all sorts of ways throughout your college life and you may not remain perfectly compatible. Getting heavily involved early on might not be the best idea. It could be very uncomfortable if it doesn't work out and it will be especially difficult if the only people you know are your ex's group of friends.
- **Relationships from college rarely last.** Sadly this is true. Even if you do feel you've found true love, the odds are that the relationship will disintegrate once you graduate and change lives once again. Sometimes clinging on to a relationship as your only stability at a time when your life is changing dramatically can seem like a good idea. It might mean you feel you ought to turn down options for your career and limit your mobility because of a tie to a relationship. Most relationships crumble within a year of graduation because of these pressures. But then, who knows, maybe your relationship will be the one that does work out.

Long-distance Lovers

For those students already involved in a relationship there are inevitable worries about how long it can last when you disappear into the distance to spend at least three years apart. First of all you're going to miss them like hell, secondly you'll only get to see each other every now and again, and thirdly can you trust them (or can they trust you) when you're out of sight and out of mind? Well, you're just going to have to wait and see. Like every other relationship, who can tell if your long-distance love will survive the miles and months you are apart? Whatever happens, make sure you don't cut yourself off from making the most of your time at college. You'll be missing out on the exciting social scene if you're disappearing every weekend to be with your heart's desire and, if the relationship does sour, you could end up feeling very alone. Expanding your overdraft with nightly calls and sobbing into your pillow won't help you to enjoy college life to the maximum. Keep things in perspective.

Lucy, at Birmingham University, found, despite the initial heartbreak, things could not have worked out better when her boyfriend from home finished with her one week before her first-year exams. 'I was devastated when he told me, especially since I was in a real state over sitting my first college exams. We'd gone out for a year before I went to college and it had been hard work keeping the relationship going on a weekend basis. But he came up from London one day just to tell me it was over and I thought he'd come up midweek because he wanted to be with me. That sort of made it worse for me because it was out of the blue, in the middle of a stressful time, and because I thought I'd tried hard to keep the relationship going – too hard, it seems now. But as soon as he'd said his bit and left I went to see my best friend who lived in another hall and we got drunk and said horrible things about him and laughed and laughed and laughed. It was great because it made me realize that I had some really great friends at college and that I wasn't totally reliant on him. I could then start going out with them at weekends instead of rushing off to the station every Friday night for the train back home. And I knew then I was going to be all right. By the end of the first week apart I'd almost stopped hating him, and by the end of the second week I'd practically forgotten him altogether.'

Hearts and Flowers and Red-hot Flushes

Enough of the bad news. You're young, you're available (or could be at a moment's notice) and then suddenly something happens. Even when you're not looking for love you become aware of the possibilities of romance right on your doorstep. There's a fair amount of beating-hearts and fluttering-eyelash moments to be had at college. Maybe it's something to do with the musty smell of library books and the scent of stale beer in the bar, but sooner or later it hits you.

Your eyes meet across a crowded library. Or you're trembling as you sit opposite them in a seminar. You're shaking in the bar, and you're on the look out for them constantly. Whenever you see them it's a nightmare and a dream come true at the same time. Your hands go clammy, your head starts spinning, your heart beats madly and you may well go bright red. It's the best feeling in the world when you find you fancy someone, but there's almost instant heartache as the tricky game of getting their attention begins.

But what to do? Clare, a second-year in London, recounts her experience of meeting the man of her dreams in the office of the student newspaper. 'I sort of started to notice this person, and then I would try to hang around if he came in. I would look out for him in the bar. I would laugh nervously at jokes he made to the crowd, but I could not look at or speak to him directly. I was a total bag of nerves. Did he like me? Was anything going to happen? It was a real nightmare and at the same time I loved it. It gave me a sense of purpose, I suppose, and I really enjoyed any few minutes I spent in his company. It made my day seem worthwhile if I managed to get in the same room as him, or could just see him in the street.'

This went on for a couple of weeks and then, at the Christmas party, he came up and spoke to her. 'God knows how I kept my cool but I did. I don't think I blushed but I probably made some pretty bad jokes. We carried on chatting through the evening. He bought me drinks, and it was going really well, I thought. Eventually by the time the bar closed we were snogging away and he asked me to go back to his room in halls, which I did.'

But the path of true love does not run smoothly, not ever, and just as Clare thought her dreams had come true it all went quite horribly wrong. 'After a night of passion, he got up, announced he was off to have a shower and asked me to leave. I did and I really didn't worry about it, I was so head over heels. But when I got back and told my friends they were furious. I'd been used. I must have been such easy prey. And then it was really difficult going into the newspaper office and seeing him and acting like nothing happened because, of course, everyone knew about it. What a disaster!'

Certainly college romances attract disaster. At the end of the day there are some bastards out there and in the steamy mist of infatuation it's hard to spot the egomaniacs who can play havoc with your heart.

Alice was a first-year who, within a fortnight of starting her course, found herself totally infatuated with a boy in her tutorial group. After a term of budding passion and a lot of trembling on her part, things finally came to a head at the Christmas Ball. But like Clare's experience, it turned out to be no more than a one-night stand and after all those days, weeks and months of anticipation and expectation she was left with the embarrassment of facing him in the corridor, in tutorials and all over the college for the next three years. 'It did get easier as time went by, but I was very embarrassed and still felt nervous whenever I was around him. Sometimes I wonder if things hadn't come to a head then, perhaps my infatuation would have continued for the whole course, or maybe I might have changed my mind. At the time I felt overwhelmingly in love with him and I couldn't think of anything else. It was an intense crush, made worse by the fact I could see him so often. It didn't work out in the end and I don't think I made a fool of myself. Nor did he, but it was very uncomfortable having to carry on studying with him for the rest of my course.'

Joy at Reading University knows what it's like to have to face the fated ex almost every day. 'The most regrettable relationship I have ever had was with someone in my hall. Despite the fact it only lasted a few days he now refuses to speak to me – which is made more difficult by the fact we are supposed to be working on a project together. Unfortunately, because we will continue to see each other for at least another two years, a certain degree of uneasiness will need to be endured.'

Stabs at romance which then turn sour can cause problems, especially if you're going to have to be in close contact with the person for the rest of your college career, be it through your group of friends or because you're on the same course and will see each other in lectures and tutorials. It can be pretty tricky trying to avoid each other in the close-knit student community and, if things have ended on bad terms, it can be awful. It might just work out, it might just be worth the risk, but remember you might be bumping into them daily for the next few years.

Even worse is when the unthinkable happens and against your better judgement you find yourself about to embark on an adventure with your flatmate and it doesn't work out to be the romance of the century. Karen, at Loughborough, has this advice: 'There are several categories of people you should never have sex with as a student. Tutors, course-mates but especially flatmates. It's so easy to forget, in the heat of the moment, that you've got to spend nine months sharing a living space with this person. If it proves to be a one-nighter you've got months of awkwardness to come, the impossibility of avoiding each other altogether and those twinges of jealousy when he brings someone else home. On the other hand, if you become an item you've got that too-much syndrome on your hands. And you miss out on that delicious getting-to-know-you stage when even the phone ringing gives you butterflies. A friend of mine made the mistake of sleeping with her flatmate. It only happened a couple of times, but according to her it was a stupid thing to do because she had to spend the next few months avoiding him and his new girlfriend, which is pretty difficult when you share a kitchen and living room with them. So the best advice when you're looking for a house is to share with other girls or, failing that, several David Mellor lookalikes, so sex will be the last thing on your mind.'

Love and Lecturers

Relationships between students and lecturers are a hot topic when they happen. And they do. Teaching staff at colleges and universities are very different from teachers at school. They treat students as adults who share their enthusiasm for the subject they teach and enjoy working with them. They are usually much more relaxed and informal and many students find they develop real friendships with their lecturers. But when sex and romance get in the picture, it can be a different story altogether.

Power is undoubtedly an aphrodisiac, and a lecturer who has all the maturity, knowledge and power so obviously lacking in your fellow students can seem amazingly attractive, despite age difference or even appearance. Similarly, you're young, bright and interested and that will certainly be in your favour.

But beware. With staff–student affairs there are the inevitable concerns over the power imbalance. After all, your tutor has the powers which could affect your course grades and there are obvious worries about favouritism (when things are going right) and revenge (when things go wrong).

Unlike school, there are no strict rules about relationships between a student and a member of university staff. However, the Association of University Teachers, the trade union for lecturers and tutors, has laid down guidelines for 'consensual relationships between staff and students'. And because they believe relationships like this 'will always involve serious risks and may involve serious difficulties rooted in the unequal power' they advise that it is the duty of the lecturer or tutor to declare the relationship to a superior member of staff or a colleague or a third party. They then advise that it should be up to another member of staff to assess the work of the student concerned to try and eliminate the possibilities of any accusations of prejudice in favour of or against the student.

But perhaps one of the worst things about staff–student relationships is the reaction of other students.

Mandy was an undergraduate at a college in London but is now studying for a postgraduate course in Oxford. She had a relationship with one of her tutors whilst she was studying for her first degree. They met through tutorials, and he was, as she puts it, 'a serial student-shagger. I wasn't the first student he had had a relationship with. We got on very well during tutorials and started going out for a drink after. Eventually I ended up sleeping with him.' The relationship went on for five months, until Mandy's course finished and she promptly left him, and went off to Oxford with a first class degree. But it was the way fellow students treated her that really concerned her, especially her friends. 'Everyone presumed that I'd only had a relationship with him to get a first class degree or that the only reason I did so well was because of him.'

Relationships are, by their very nature, very individual things. There are no hard and fast rules about how to play the game of love while you're at college. The *Cosmo* Student Advisory Board has some cautionary tales and some sound advice which cover just about all the common predicaments of college romance.

- 'I was single when I arrived at university. A few of those with partners at home are still together in their third year, but almost all of those relationships died a death before the end of the first year.'
- 'Some people instantly latch on to a person before the end of their first week, and they stay together for months, even years. Perhaps this is brought on by the enormity of the strange alien world they are facing. Perhaps they are just lucky. For my own part I am glad I managed to avoid doing that, no matter how reassuring it would have seemed at the time.'
- 'I was single through most of my university career, and I am glad of it really, as I have done far more than I would have done otherwise. My boyfriend and I are two intensely independent people who choose to spend their lives together, rather than two people who stay together because they could not manage on their own. I prefer it that way.'
- 'When you first fall for someone at university, it's so easy to be so swept along by the added dimension of "freedom" that you completely overlook what you're getting yourself into. You can sleep together whenever you want, which means he'll always be over at your house because you're the one with the food and your place is always tidier. Quickly, you end up shopping for two, cooking for two, putting his washing with yours, typing up his essays, lending him money and sorting out his problems.'

- 'Don't rush into anything serious, especially in the first term. So often people get together with someone in the first few weeks and everything's fine until the relationship ends and they find that they don't know anyone at university apart from their ex-boyfriend and his friends. However great the new bloke in your life is you should also remember the old saying that whereas boyfriends come and go, friends will be around much longer.'
- 'Try to avoid getting involved with someone you live with. One of my friends did and when the relationship ended the atmosphere got so bad she had to move out.'
- 'I met my boyfriend at the end of freshers fortnight. He was quite a bit older than me and a final-year student, although inexperienced, like me, when it came to relationships. We've been together for just over two years. At first, although we technically lived apart – me in halls, him outside – by the end of the year we felt as though we were living together. By the end of the first year we had grown so much together we were very serious about each other and had to start preparing ourselves for a long-distance relationship as he left college to go back to his home town. It was weird going back to college without him in my second year but we survived, but only just in some instances. Recently the relationship has become more open in that I'm bisexual and we have an arrangement so that we can see other people, with me principally other women, but it has spread to other men.'
- 'It's tempting to live in each other's pockets, share a house, meals, washing, be a total couple. Personally I'd say go slow on the domesticated bit. You've got three years to be young, free and have fun, and about three decades to be domesticated – if you ever want to be. You can still have your cake and eat in bed, but you don't need to argue about whose turn it is to wash the sheets just yet.'
- 'Everything seems to happen much faster than in the real world. Outside college I would never consider inviting a guy I'd only spoken to that night in the bar to stay over. Somehow when you are at college, and you know he is too, you feel safer. One-night stands within a "big happy family community" are acceptable, and it might turn out to be love at first sight. Yeah, and you won't have

an overdraft in three years. Maybe, just maybe, it will work out and in ten years' time you'll be shopping in Sainsbury's with junior in the trolley, blissfully happy. All the same, be careful. Use protection goes without saying, but sometimes you need a rubber for your heart too.'

- 'The most defining thing about living in a student house or halls is that everyone knows when everyone else is having sex. It can be really embarrassing when you come downstairs flushed and obviously post-coital and your friends have all been sitting there for the past half hour watching the lampshade swing and putting the TV back against the wall occasionally.'
- 'If you get yourself into any sort of relationship where there might be something for people around college to gossip about and spread rumours, be prepared that the gossip will probably happen, no matter how careful you are. I know from experience how rapidly rumours can get around a department, for example.'

At the end of the day, your love life at college is going to be as difficult to manage as your bank account. It is a difficult time because of the pressures of study and the continuous process of change and development you and any of your partners will go through. Enjoy the exploration and the evolution but look after your heart and you will be sure to live to love another day if and when it all goes wrong.

Chapter 7 / **Making Your Mark and Making the Most of Your College Life**

They say your student days are the best days of your life and that being at college is about much more than getting drunk, getting overdrawn and studying for exams. If you really want to make the most of your student days, it pays to take advantage of all the other opportunities on offer on top of the lectures and cheap bars. There are so many opportunities to do the things you've always dreamt of doing, to make your mark, discover new things about yourself, challenge yourself, learn new skills, as well as make really good friends along the way.

Joy at Reading University found that getting involved in extra-curricular college activities was the making of her social life. 'There are so many people beginning university each year that the choice of friends "available" is huge. However, there are lots of opportunities to meet people through various groups and I have met a wide range of people through things such as the student paper, drama productions and the student council. It means that you are not limited to one circle of people, although close friends are really the most important.'

Getting involved in other activities will not only help your future career in terms of those extra CV Brownie points, it can also open up new areas of interest, teach you new skills and give you a whole new network of friends. College life is designed around providing you with hundreds of extra-curricular activities, whether your interests are creative, political or just about keeping fit and doing something different outside of the library and the student union bar.

Miranda at De Montfort University says, 'There are opportunities at university which you may never get anywhere else. If you want to play women's rugby, try your hand at being the next Lisa l'Anson on the student radio station, direct a production of *Grease* or edit the student newspaper, then go for it. These days you need to have more on your CV than a good degree, so getting involved is important.'

Miranda is convinced that getting involved in student activities makes a real difference to your motivation and to enjoying student life. 'This year, driven by nostalgic memories of running around muddy hockey pitches on freezing Saturday mornings and a new-academic-year resolution to get fit, I signed up as a member of the hockey club. It has turned out to be one of the best decisions I've made whilst I've been at university. Not only am I much fitter, but I've also made loads of new friends and my social life has improved no end. So far this year there have been bowling and paintballing trips and a hockey-club party as well as numerous nights out where drinking games play a crucial part of the proceedings. In the Easter vacation we're going on a hockey tour to the Isle of Man. All new students should get involved in a club or society which interests them, and if there isn't one, you can start your own. Not only do you meet loads more people, but it can also help you feel a real part of the university.'

Most colleges and universities run a wide range of activities, usually through the student union. And if there isn't a club or society for your particular interest you can easily start one up by getting together a few people and applying to the student union for funding for equipment, meeting spaces and help with organization and promotion. There's normally a clubs and societies officer at each student union who can give you advice on how to go about setting up your own club.

Getting yourself involved is easy. Choosing what to do can be more of a task, and you might well find that whatever you decide to do leads you into other things, especially if you get involved in the organizational side of your activity.

The opportunities are endless. Here's a taster of just some of the pastimes on offer to while away those moments between lectures and last orders. Anyone can do it, whatever your course of study, no experience necessary. This is your chance to have a go at anything and everything, make the most of your free time and make a mark for yourself.

- hockey
- hang-gliding
- learning to fly
- writing for student magazines
- putting on bands and discos
- being in a band
- DJ-ing
- presenting a programme on student radio
- putting on a play
- acting in a play
- designing sets and costumes
- Latin American dancing
- tap dancing
- putting on a dance show
- putting on a fashion show for charity
- community action work
- charity fund-raising
- organizing a ball
- politics/running for election
- running a women's group
- debating
- rugby
- chess
- campaigning
- photography
- sub-aqua
- opera
- life-saving
- film-making
- mountaineering
- meditation
- setting up a student TV station

The possibilities are limitless. It's up to you to get going and get involved. You may not have the chance again, and this might be the move that changes your life. Often students who get involved in extra-curricular activities at college find out they really enjoy it and go on to pursue careers in the field. There's only one way to find out.

Student Unions

Getting involved in the student union is very easy and, since student union activities are so diverse, there are many opportunities to do something that really interests you, from running social events to running for office as one of the student union's elected officers, and all the rewards and responsibilities that go with that. You could end up running the place.

Most activities centre round the student union, or student guild or association, and student unions are responsible for running most clubs and societies as well as all the social and welfare services on offer to students.

Every member of the college is automatically a member of their student union and has the right to influence its decisions, elect the representative officers and get involved in the organization. Usually student unions have a number of full-time elected student officers – the sabbaticals – who have either taken a year out of their studies or just finished their course. Their job is to represent the views of the students to the college and to run the various aspects of the student union services, oversee the union's finances and help other students. Often there will be a president, a finance officer, a welfare officer, and in many cases there will be a sports officer, an entertainments officer and a publications or communications officer. They work alongside a team of elected student representatives, the Executive, who will be non-sabbaticals and will be fitting in their student union work alongside their studies. They will represent the views of various groups of students, so, for example, there's usually a women's officer, an international students' officer, a postgraduate students' officer, a halls officer (representing students in halls of residence), and other representative officers.

Many colleges also have a Student Representative Council which works with the Executive and the sabbaticals. Usually each department or course elects a student representative to take their views to the Student Representative Council and to vote on their behalf on important matters, and determine policy.

Some student unions still run General Meetings, where all the students can turn up and vote on matters important to the student community. The subjects up for discussion can be wide-ranging. It might be about something like hall fees being increased and organizing student opposition, campaigning for a new library or extended library hours, improving access for students with disabilities or it might be on matters more to do with the union itself, and holding the officers accountable for their work.

Some decisions will also be made by a cross-campus referendum, and every student will be given the opportunity to vote at ballot boxes across the campus. Almost all the student unions in the country are affiliated to the National Union of Students and students will be given the opportunity to decide whether or not their student union should affiliate in a cross-campus ballot.

Cross-campus ballots ae also used to elect the student union officers, and the students who will represent your student union at the NUS National Conference. Elections for all the various positions within the student union are usually held just before Easter, and all students can vote. All students are entitled to stand for election as well. You will need to produce a manifesto outlining what you plan to do if you win the election and you will have to get together some friends to help with canvassing students and persuading them to vote for you.

Getting involved in running your student union and the union's activities can be tremendously rewarding and certainly gives you the opportunity to learn some very useful skills, from running meetings and public speaking through to budgeting, negotiating and producing publicity. It also gives you the opportunity to do something for yourself and your fellow students, whether it's getting better bands to appear, getting a new crèche, producing a newspaper or campaigning for better lighting on campus. It can be tiring and exhausting work and certainly you'll need a determined spirit and a whole lot of enthusiasm, but there is real team spirit and it is a great way to meet like-minded people, not just from your college but from neighbouring colleges and colleges across the country.

Helping Other People

Many students derive a great deal of personal satisfaction out of helping others, and there are several ways to use your free time to help others within the student community and beyond, and to pick up some useful skills along the way. Most student unions run a Nightline service for students. This is a phone line that runs throughout the night and is there as an opportunity for students who are lonely, depressed or troubled to call in confidence. The Nightline service will be staffed by anonymous student volunteers who receive training beforehand.

Another way to get involved in helping others is through Student Community Action. Student Community Action groups give students the opportunity to focus their energies into helping the local community through a whole range of different activities, from working with local children or disadvantaged groups to environmental work. The work of Student Community Action groups has a real benefit to the local community and also helps to build bridges between the townsfolk and students, who are often seen in a bad light by the locals.

One huge way in which students work together to help others, by way of having a very good time, is through Rag, the traditional week of charity fund-raising. Virtually every college in the country has a Rag Week, and it's a long, long tradition in college life. Some of the more elaborate Rag high-jinks and mad capers have died a death, outlawed by the police or the college activities, but it is still a week of serious partying and fund-raising. Expect a Rag Ball, beer festivals, sponsored hitch-hikes, collecting in the streets in full fancy dress, fashion shows, custard-pie hit squads (where you pay a team of custard pie throwers to attack your innocent friends and enemies), a Rag mag (containing some horrendous jokes) and a whole diary of mad events, all in the name of charity.

A Rag committee will be elected or pulled together from eager volunteers each year to organize the timetable of events and to work with the charities. Rag can generate huge amounts of money and the organization of a campus-wide week of frolics can take many months. Rag, other charity work, community action and Nightline are brilliant opportunities to challenge yourself and develop skills while helping other people.

Sports

Sport at college is for everyone. Of course, there are those who take sport very seriously and you can get involved in competing on a national and international level through inter-college tournaments, but a lot of people get involved for fun and for fitness. Sports aren't confined to school favourites either. Alongside the traditional 'girl' sports of netball, hockey, tennis, gymnastics and swimming, there's often rowing, women's rugby, women's football, skiing, volleyball, athletics, squash, riding, polo, water-polo, fencing, sailing and a whole range of more unusual sporting pursuits. Clubs often have professional trainers and coaches, and team members usually train at least once a week. Sporting tournaments are traditionally held on Wednesday afternoons, the sacred window in the college diary left free for sport and other more leisurely activities. There are often matches and games on Saturday afternoons. Most clubs also organize a whole timetable of social activities throughout the term for those all-important team bonding sessions (which usually involve alcohol to some extent).

Most clubs also organize tours abroad and matches at other

colleges across the country, so you can climb aboard the team bus and see the world. Student sport is definitely a great way to get fit, make friends and have fun all at the same time.

Clubs are oganized with captains, presidents, treasurers and secretaries from within the team and you can easily get involved in helping run and organize your college club. Most people find getting involved in helping run the team is very rewarding and, of course, it will go down well on your CV, and you can pick up all-important skills such as time-management, working in a team and organizational skills, which will impress your future employers no end.

Clubs and Societies

Non-sporting clubs and societies are prolific and diverse. They cover everything from cultural and religious groups for students with similar interests or similar backgrounds to meet, through to political and campaigning groups, to hobbies and pastimes, like chess or meditation. The clubs usually meet weekly or fortnightly and organize social activities as well as meetings.

Your student union can help you set up a club if one doesn't exist already, but most big colleges and universities have most areas covered by now. The political societies, such as Labour Clubs, the Liberal Democrats, Conservatives or Greens, have national support, debate issues and help with campaigning. If you have a yearning for a political career someday, this is a great way to get involved and influence things from the grassroots. Campaigning and support groups, such as women's groups, or lesbian, gay and bisexual groups, work closely with the student union usually, helping to organize special events and campaigns and representing those groups on campus as well as providing support and social events.

Other campaigning groups, such as animal rights or environmental groups, give you the opportunity to put your concerns into action, and raise the profile of issues that concern you and they often organize debates and open meetings. Religious and cultural groups offer support for students from similar backgrounds and give students the chance to meet together and discuss their interests in their own culture or religion. Other clubs and societies are more about hobbies and interests, from the film society (which organizes film screenings) and drama society or dance society (which puts on plays and performances and gives students the chance to act, direct, produce, chroeograph, design sets, costumes and lighting) to debating societies and games societies (like chess or bridge). They all give you the chance to have a go at something new and enjoy indulging your interests with like-minded people. National and international competitions offer the opportunity to pit your skills against colleges and universities from across the country and across the globe.

Debating

The ancient student pursuit of debating is still as popular as ever and continues to impress even the most complacent employer trawling through piles of graduate CVs. It is a great way to polish up your public speaking and develop the art of argument. Debating usually takes place in teams and every subject under the sun has been covered at some time by a student debate, and teams compete across the country.

Student Drama

Drama is a traditional and still thriving student pastime and college performances are the breaking ground for much new talent. You don't have to have experience to join in, just enthusiasm. Whether you're a behind-the-scenes character or the original extrovert you'll find a role for yourself somewhere. Many of today's famous names made the big break in student performances. Many college drama societies put on several performances each term, covering all kinds of theatre. As well as the classic plays and lavish musicals, there are student productions of lesser-known plays and even new plays written by students. Every year student groups have the chance to take their plays and productions to the Edinburgh Fringe Festival and impress an international audience and possibly some talent scouts. There's also a National Student Drama Festival each year, profiling new student plays. If you ever had the urge to tread the boards or slap on some grease-paint, then student drama gives you the biggest chance in your life to have a go on a grand scale (or even on a small scale) and have a laugh at the same time.

Student Journalism

Student media have really taken off in recent years. They have always been seen as the breeding ground for new journalists, and if you ever want a job even slightly connected with the media, this is the place to start. It is also a great way to find out if you can do it and if you enjoy doing it. Even if you have no intention of pursuing a media career then you can at least indulge your creative impulses and pick up very useful skills which can't fail to impress. Working to deadlines, working in a team, and using your initiative and imagination are all part and parcel of student media and are skills that will be usefully honed for whatever you decide to do next.

The advent of desk-top publishing means student media are now being produced in-house to incredibly high standards. Most colleges have at least one student magazine or newspaper, and many now produce specialist magazines, such as a law students magazine, or medics, or an arts magazine, and there are also a growing number of radio and TV stations.

Getting involved is easy. If you want to write, edit, take photos, produce, present, research, review, mix, design or layout, then all you have to do is turn up and volunteer your services. In many established student media operations the team structure is quite hierarchical and those who have been there longest and have the most experience will help newcomers with equipment and training and teach you the tricks of the trade. With some, however, it's more a case of all hands to the pumps and it will be a case of picking it up as you go along.

If you want to set up a new publication or station then you should approach your student union for help with funding, equipment and office space. They may ask for something in return, such as advertising space for discos and gigs and coverage of student union events and services, but many will be more than willing to help set up and support a new venture. The NUS produces a handbook, *The Student Media Handbook*, which gives advice on getting advertising, design, libel law, researching your audience and everything you need to know about setting up new student media.

If you've dreamt of shouting 'hold the front page', or of interviewing politicians, photographing pop stars, designing double-page spreads or reading the news, then this is your big chance, as student media know no limits in their cheekiness and opportunity-grabbing tactics. They give so much scope to any would-be news hound, paparazzo, columnist, critic, editor, producer or presenter to do as much as they want. If you have the initiative, the imagination and the drive then you can make your mark. Student media are also a great team activity (all those late nights meeting deadlines and brainstorming for ideas) and a thriving atmosphere for mutual creativity. You can make great friends and find real inspiration from other people's ideas and enthusiasm. The *Guardian* NUS Student Media Awards is the prestigious national competition each year for the best student newspaper, magazine, TV and radio station and it is well worth entering your particular publication or station for that extra accolade.

Whatever you opt to do with your free time it pays to make the most of the opportunities. It may be your chance to find your true vocation, it will almost certainly help you develop new skills and find out more about yourself and your own capabilities, it is a great way to meet like-minded people and to have fun and it will definitely make your time at college more worthwhile. This is your chance to make your mark and make the most of your time at college.

Chapter 8 / **Travel and Making the Most of Vacations**

As every student knows, you're the luckiest people alive when it comes to the summer. Months of empty bliss stretch before you and what to do with them is one of the nicest dilemmas going. Exams, essays and accommodation hassles can be put on hold and you even have the opportunity to reduce your overdraft dramatically. Making the most of the long summer vacations is well worth the while. Out there in the real world people are restricted to just two weeks' break from the routine of life but right now you have months to play with. The options are to travel, work, or loll around at home enjoying the luxuries of a house with real windows and a fully stocked fridge. But if you plan it right you could fit in all three and still have time on your hands to free your mind and spirit ready for the next term.

The idea of spending all your time back in the luxury of home is usually quickly dismissed after a few days of pampering, and plans for adventure and earning get put into action. Many students, especially first-years returning home for their first big vacation, find it something of a shock to try and readjust to the routine of family life after the libertarian student lifestyle.

Helen, at Cambridge, sums it up. 'Being with Mummy and Daddy during the holidays can come as a huge shock after your first taste of independence. I found that the best way to deal with this is to spend as little time at home as possible. It sounds harsh, but I would prefer to spend a week with my family getting on with them and enjoying their company than be there for a month and argue bitterly because you're feeling trapped. So go and visit friends, go abroad if you can afford it, claim that you have to go back early because of work, and really make the most of the time you spend at home.'

Kirsty, at Oxford University, says, 'The best thing about the vacation is the worst thing too: being at home again. It's a rest, a great opportunity to catch up with old friends and family, but after five days you're hankering after getting back to college. Then you realize just how lucky you are to have a choice between the two worlds. The best thing about being a student is having so many choices.'

Joy at Reading comments, 'Holidays are so long that it is really worthwhile making the most of them. Up until now I have used the time to work and now have enough saved to travel for the whole summer vacation this year. Reading through guidebooks and choosing my destination is a current hobby and I am looking forward to spending three months in either Eastern Europe, India or the Far East – a shortened list of possibilities.'

Most students like to spend at least some of the summer travelling and holidaying. And the travel companies know it. There are now quite a few travel companies specializing in student deals and arranging trips for independent travellers. The competition for students' hard-earned cash (and overdrafts) is fierce and there are real bargains to be had. Most colleges have a branch of a student travel company on campus and you'll find a student travel shop in every university town and city. Look out for details of the latest student deals in your college newspaper or magazine or pop into your campus branch for a flick through some brochures and a look at the prices. Things couldn't be better for students. Not only do you have tons of time to spare but there are fantastic discounts on travel by train, plane, bus and sea to destinations across the world.

Your NUS card will suffice for booking discounts in Britain but if you are going abroad it's well worth your while investing in an International Student Identity Card for discounts and deals on admission prices, train tickets, flights and bus journeys all over the world.

Deciding what to do, when to do it, where to go and who with are easy problems to solve. Maybe you want to earn some cash with a summer job and then try a spot of island-hopping in Greece. Or perhaps an inter-rail trip taking in all the European cities plus a few beaches takes your fancy. Or the States, or South-East Asia or India. The options are endless.

Exotic locations, cultural expeditions, new horizons, foreign soil and tropical sunshine beckon. This is your chance to get out and explore, live a different life for a short while, meet new people and have a wild, wild time.

However you choose to do it, travelling can be a real eye-opener and despite inevitable minor disasters and catastrophes, you can have a proper adventure on very little money.

Becky, from London, toured France and Italy by train (with a spot of hitch-hiking thrown in) with a college friend. 'We worked for about four weeks just temping but managed to save up a couple of hundred pounds to see us through the rest of the summer. We planned to find work grape-picking or working on the beaches if we did run out of money. We had the time of our lives and some real adventures. We got into some amazing scrapes, and took some dodgy risks, which I don't think I'd do again. But by the end of the summer we had met some really interesting people, polished up our languages, seen some real sights and we'd spent hardly any money. It was just us, our rucksacks, a tent and a mission to explore. It was really good fun. I'll never forget swimming in Sicily or the beach barbecues in the South of France and it was great to arrive back at college full of stories of our adventures and with a tan.'

If you are strapped for cash but still have wanderlust, it might be worth taking the option of a working holiday. In exchange for work on an American or Canadian summer camp you can expect the reward of a free return flight with a few weeks spare to travel in North America after your toils on the camp are complete. It's an option many students find perfect in these poverty-stricken times and summer camps enthusiastically pursue British students to entertain the kids.

If working your way around foreign climes seems like the solution to your funding problems whilst fulfilling your desire to see the world (or at least part of it), there are several books worth getting hold of from the library or checking out in the careers office. Vacation Work (01865 241978) publish three which are really worthwhile reads for would-be travellers: *Work Your Way Around the World*, *The Directory of Summer Jobs Abroad*, and for those keen to see the States, there's *Summer Jobs USA*. Educational publishers Kogan Page produce the *Guide to Working Abroad*, which is also full of facts and advice on selling your services in foreign parts.

Working while you're away can also be a good way to experience the culture of a place and to mix with the locals in a way most tourists never enjoy. The International Voluntary Service (01206 298215) has information on voluntary work at centres across the globe and might be just the ticket if you feel you can donate your services for free in return for rewarding work and the chance to go native.

But wherever you decide to go, be sure you're safe. It's no good just hopping on the next plane, train or hovercraft to some tropical climate without a bit of preparation and forethought for your own health and safety. More travellers return suffering from illnesses picked up on their travels than those who return encased in plaster or transported by stretcher after an accident abroad. Students and all independent travellers like to do things on the cheap and live rough, usually out of necessity rather than a disdain for four-star hotels. But with that there are certain risks involved, so before you travel anywhere wise up on the climes, customs and common diseases currently rife in your dream destinations. Get hold of an up-to-date guidebook for independent travellers, such as those published by Lonely Planet or Rough Guides, which contain in-depth information on all aspects of the countries, all recently researched by fellow-travellers on the cheap. Don't forget to visit your doctor and health clinic, not just for jabs and pills to prevent those nasty diseases but for advice on staying healthy in foreign climes.

Tips for Healthy Travelling

- Find out about the health risks in the country you are visiting. You may need vaccinations, special health-care documentation or extra medical insurance. You can get the necessary information from the student travel office or the embassy of the country concerned.
- Consult your doctor or college health clinic as soon as you can to arrange for any vaccinations, prescriptions or advice you might need. Some vaccinations have to be staggered or taken at certain stages before you go, so get advice as early as possible.
- Take a small first-aid kit: a packet of adhesive dressings, insect repellent, antiseptic cream and water-sterilization tablets should suffice for most minor hazards.
- Check that drinking water is safe. If you are unsure, either boil the water, use water-sterilization tablets or buy bottled water. Make sure that ice cubes too are made with clean water or avoid ice in your drinks.
- Be careful with foods. Raw vegetables and fruit should be washed in clean water. Raw shellfish or uncooked, reheated or cold meats can all be contaminated. If in doubt, stick to freshly cooked foods.
- Avoid heat exhaustion and sunburn. Expose yourself gradually to the sun and use sun creams of a protection factor suited to your skin type. Don't use a lower factor in the hope that you'll tan quicker – you won't. Drink plenty of non-alcoholic fluid and wear loose, lightweight clothing, preferably natural fibres.
- Take precautions to avoid bites from insects. Use insect-repellent creams and keep arms and legs covered after dusk. If you're travelling in a malaria-infested country, make sure you take the tablets and take them properly (which includes finishing the course when you get home).
- Keep a note on your person of any significant medical condition affecting you.

When you come home you should:
- Tell the doctor which countries you have visited or travelled through if you become ill after your return.
- Consult the doctor if you had any medical treatment while you were away.
- If you go to donate blood you must tell the staff if you have visited a tropical country or had any medical treatment abroad.

But not everyone is as lucky when it comes to spending the summer in idyllic relaxation or in epic exploration of some foreign shore. For more and more students, the option for travel comes only after hard graft to recoup the missing funds from their bank accounts to get them out of the red and through the next term. Make sure you know all the facts about tax and National Insurance (see the chapter on money for details of getting a job) if you are going to be working through the vacations and make sure you do get at least some chance of a rest and a chance to recharge your batteries.

Charlie, from Royal Holloway, worked her way through the summer. 'I just couldn't afford to go on holiday. I had so many debts. So I wrote to all the banks in my Easter holidays and the Midland took me on as Standing Order and Statement Clerk, but the job was so boring. But I paid off all my debts and also learnt that if you write a rude letter to the bank, you'll always get your money back. So at least I got something out of it.'

The college vacations are the longest you'll ever get so make the most of the time and the huge discounts available because these opportunities just don't exist in the big wide world beyond the college gates. Even if you have to spend some of the summer working, try and get away and enjoy one of the best sides of student life.

Chapter 9 / **Getting Ahead – Graduation and Beyond**

Just when you start to love it you realize you're going to have to leave it. Like all good things, your college course will eventually come to an end and hopefully, pending the trivial details like exam results, you'll be left clutching a certificate of success and a bank statement of an overdrawn account, with the big wide world of possibilities open before you.

It's a prettty scary thought. It wakes you up in the middle of the night. What are you going to do next? Where will you live? Who will your friends be? Just when you'd got settled into your college life you've got to start thinking about what to do in the future, and the future is creeping nearer every day.

But the time to start thinking about what to do next can't be too soon. You need to start making plans about life after graduation long before the day you throw your mortarboard in the air and shake hands with the vice-chancellor. These days the world of work or further study is hugely competitive and if you know what you want, you've got to go out and get it before everyone else does.

You may decide that you want to do further study and more and more graduates are now pursuing postgraduate courses, some for the extra qualifications to get a step ahead, some for the love of their subject and some for development and training for their chosen career. Options for postgraduate study and training are as varied as undergraduate courses, but the race for places and the competition for funding is seriously fierce.

Or you may decide now's the time to travel and broaden your horizons before you settle into a proper career and a 'grown-up' lifestyle. Many shun the prospect of mortgages, rush-hours and salaries for sun, sea and foreign shores, knowing that the extra experience and personal development they'll gain will make them an even more exciting proposition to a future employer when they do return to so-called normal life. For you maybe life is too short to step straight from study to career and you need time to work out what to do and see a few sights along the way. Working as a volunteer abroad, travelling the world, meeting new people and opening your eyes to new cultures, even learning new languages, can be exhilarating as well as hugely beneficial to your CV.

Or maybe you've had enough of student life, of roughing it in hedonistic poverty, and living in cold, damp bedsits while scraping together pennies for a few drinks in the union bar. Maybe now's the time to get your foot on the first rung of the career ladder and start working your way to the top. Options for graduate careers are now notoriously limited but even if you can't bag a corporate graduate post you can go out and find a related job in the field you're interested in.

Whatever you eventually decide to do, the chances are you'll have to debate the pros and cons of all three directions at some stage before you graduate. The art of successful graduation is to give yourself plenty of time to work out the possibilities of what you could do next and make your own opportunities.

At your earliest possible opportunity you should pay a visit to the college careers office. Their library will be stacked with information on graduate careers, on options for further study, on career training, on setting up your own business even. You can book a personal appointment with a careers counsellor, who can help point you in the right direction in terms of further information, contacts with professional bodies, training and how to apply for the job of your dreams. They can run you through databases, work out what might be suitable for you in terms of jobs you never dreamed of or never dreamed you could do, and help you with ideas for putting together your CV, filling in applications and sparkling at interviews. If you can get to see them at least a year before you graduate you'll be making moves in the right direction to sorting out a plan for your life beyond the college gates and you'll get inspired and informed on all the opportunities available.

Helen, an English student at Cambridge, explains. 'Approaching graduation is probably the most daunting time in your life so far. For the first time the chances are that you don't know exactly what you are going to do next. Part of the problem here is that lots of people do purely academic subjects which do not necessarily lead straight into a specific career. I think that more specifically vocational postgraduate studies are the way forward. The most important thing is to work out what you really want to do. If you know that and you have enough energy and enthusiasm, then you really can't fail.'

Postgraduate Study

These days more and more graduates are staying put in academe. It's not just the smell of libraries and the love of halls of residence that keeps them coming back for more. The range of courses and options has really blossomed, whether you want to take on a one-year postgraduate teaching course, or study journalism, pick up on the latest in computing to pave the way for a glittering career or delve deeper into your subject just for the love of it. There's a multitude of choices available at colleges across the country and a number of postgraduate colleges which cater especially for those who have already done the fresher party waterfights and late-night scene and want to get down to some serious studying.

If you think postgraduate possibilities could entice you into a year or so more of essay deadlines and hard graft by lamplight, the first thing you should do is find out about options for funding. The money available is sadly limited. While you will get a grant for the Postgraduate Certificate in Education (PGCE) if you want to go into teaching, you'll find funding, for both maintenance and tuition, is sadly lacking for most other postgraduate courses. There are, however, bursaries, scholarships, trusts and sponsorships available and if you're doing research you may get paid by the college in return for some undergraduate teaching.

Waste no time in finding out about all the different options for funding as the competition for cash is a lottery and the earlier you find out about the rules, regulations and often bizarre excuses surrounding the awarding of funds to a select and lucky few the better your chance of walking away with a cheque. Your first port of call should be your careers office at college, which can furnish you with information on applications for both courses and funds and point you in the right direction of scholarships, sponsors, bursaries and grant-awarding bodies. There are nine main award-making bodies for postgraduate awards – the research councils – and applications are usually made through the college department where you intend to study. The amount varies according to the subject you study. You will usually be expected to have at least an upper second honours degree but competition is so fierce even first class students may find it difficult to get funding.

If you're thinking of carrying on an aspect of the subject you're studying at undergraduate level, you should see your tutor as soon as possible. They will know all the scams and scholarships available in the subject and you'll be surprised at the obscurity of some. They will also be able to advise on the best courses and the best colleges and through their contacts they will know who would be the expert in the particular field who might be able to help you. You might find that funding for courses, if not actually getting on the course, will be dependent on your degree results and you may need your tutor to prepare a reference for you. The sooner you tell them the greater their chances of helping you prepare for applications. You will find that your tutor will be very helpful and certainly very proud to find her student has taken such an interest in her subject and is enthusiastic to pursue further study. Use her support and enthusiasm to help you find the course you want and the funding you need.

There are few hard and fast rules about applying for postgraduate courses. Find out what's available first and work out what you'd like to do as soon as you can and then do as much research and groundwork as you can to work your way through the maze of applications for both places and funds.

Andrea, doing postgraduate research in politics at Queen's University in Belfast, is enthusiastic about the plus points of further study after a first degree. 'To anyone thinking of postgraduate work, I'd say definitely go for it. An increase in the number of people leaving university with a primary degree and higher expectations from employers means that having a postgraduate qualification should improve your chances in the market place, especially if you're learning skills, like IT, that you can bring to a new job. Even if you are doing an "arts" thesis, like an M.Phil., it still shows potential employers that you have not only the ability, but also the determination and tenacity, to prove that you're a success.'

However, there are down sides to a few more years in amongst the text books and musty libraries, and, despite the love of the subject, if your postgraduate study has no obvious vocational direction, there's that sneaky feeling that you might be perceived as just delaying the decision-making. As Andrea explains, 'The only drawback to doing a postgraduate course is that it's left me even more confused about what to do next. I don't know if employers will appreciate the fact that I've got a higher degree or be suspicious that at the age of twenty-five I still don't seem to be on a "traditional" career path. I love the work I'm doing, but I'm quite concerned about my future prospects, and I'm torn between really enjoying the research I'm doing for my thesis and feeling the need to get on the first rung of the career ladder as soon as possible.'

But most employers will appreciate and, in fact, applaud your years of extra study and the efforts that have put you ahead of your class-mates. You've been broadening your mind and developing even more as well as showing dedication to your ambitions. Even the most strait-laced graduate employer will be happy to take on a well-rounded individual and will see your extra qualifications and further study as a bonus. They certainly won't be put off by a few more letters after your name and the fact that you're a few years older than some of their straight-from-college applicants.

In Search of the Perfect Job

In years gone by the employers came knocking on the doors of the college begging for graduates, waving cheques and the keys to a company car. Or so legend has it. The 'milk round', as it was once known, whereby the big companies toured the so-called best universities, hunting down finalists with promises of big bucks and glamorous jobs, has gone sour and there are now very few companies actively seeking large numbers of graduate recruits. These days, if you want work, you're going to have to go out and get it and getting it is not easy.

The joke that started doing the rounds on campus when the first shock of graduate unemployment statistics hit the headlines was 'What do you say to a graduate with a job? A Big Mac and fries, please.' Unfortunately it's hardly stretching the boundaries of the reality of the situation today. There are plenty of graduates working in bars, shops, pubs and restaurants to earn an honest living and they are certainly not using their talents to the full.

But don't get down, get determined. Make an early start and know your field. It is possible to get work and to make moves on a possible career. These days graduates have to accept that they will have to start at the bottom of the ladder and take as many opportunities as possible to get a foot in the door rather than find someone offers them the manager's desk on their first day of work.

Research, determination, persistence and experience will pay off. Start making plans to make yourself more employable now and you'll find your chances of landing a job are seriously improved. There's a lot you can do whilst still a student to stand you in good stead for gainful employment in the future. You have to make sure you will shine above the rest.

What to Do Now

Polish up your chances of success by doing as much now to give you the edge in terms of skills, experience and CV-sparkle. Here are some ways of doing just that:

- Join clubs and societies if they interest you. Your future employers will be looking for evidence that you have not spent the best three years of your life locked up in books and bars. Evidence of responsibility in a club or society will impress. Develop organizational skills as the club secretary, arranging meetings and members and ensuring meetings run to schedule. Polish up your talents as a team leader as the chair or captain. Even if these skills are not essential to your chosen career, employers will realize that they can enhance the way you will approach work, such as being part of a team or working to deadlines, and they are proof of your commitment to learning outside your academic studies. They want proof of decision-making and entrepreneurial skills, so, even while you're getting involved in raising money through Rag Week, you'll be earning CV Brownie points.
- Pick up new vocational skills. If you want to be a journalist, get involved in student media. It's a brilliant way to gain the sort of experience and technical know-how that most hopefuls can gain only through years of slog. At college you get the chance to do things like student broadcasting, film-making, producing and directing for free and for fun and you can learn crucial skills which will set you above the others in a very competitive recruitment field. There are plenty of opportunities to explore your creative potential and prove that you can do anything you set your mind to.
- Learn a language, brush up your rusty GCSE French or try your hand at something new like Japanese. Learn to type, learn how to work a computer. All these courses are on offer for free while you're still a student and most colleges will offer beginners sessions at lunch-time or to fit in around your lectures.

Take advantage of it now. They cost big money in the real world.
- Do your research now. Draw up a list of target companies and organizations and read the trade journals in the field. Find out who are big operators, who are up-and-coming, the movers, the shakers and the hot issues in the industry. You have to know what you're getting into and the extra information will help no end when it comes to applications and interviews.
- Make contacts now. Find out who you need to know. Write to them and ask for work experience. It's not who you know but who knows you that counts. Get out there and make yourself known. Build up a network of contacts through work experience and keep in touch. Try getting part-time work in a related field, to get experience and contacts while earning the cash you need to see you through college.
- Find out from possible future employers just what they want in a new recruit. Call the big companies and ask to speak to the personnel department. They will be only too happy to help out, and can supply you with all the corporate literature and details of application procedures. With smaller companies and organizations, write to the top dog and ask for advice on getting into the field. Even if they don't have vacancies or opportunities for you they will be happy to point you in the right direction and advise you on who to go to for a foot in the door. Be polite, persistent and enthusiastic. Don't be a nuisance and understand that you're obviously not the priority for them – these are busy and successful career people. Most will be flattered by the interest you show and will be happy to help as much as they can so long as you don't become a pain. These contacts will pay off and will certainly give you the inside edge and the information you need to set you off.
- Start working on your CV now. Look at what's lacking and polish up your plus points. Get advice and make sure it looks good. But whatever you do, don't go overboard on the fonts, fancy gimmicks and other wonders of the word processor. Most of all, make sure it reads well and that there are no mistakes. Don't

rely on the computer spell-check but get it looked over by at least two literate people to make sure there are no glaring errors and howling typos.

Andrea at Queen's reveals the realities of shoddy applications and warns of the pitfalls. 'I've done some secretarial temping for large companies in the past and I'm amazed at the number of CVs that are sent in with spelling mistakes, grammatical errors and even suspicious-looking stains on the pages. I can't believe people think an employer is going to leap up and offer them a job on that basis. Whatever you do before you send it off, double check your CV for spelling, grammar, layout and design – then get a friend to check it over. She'll be able to cast an objective eye over it and then you can check it again yourself. Don't sell yourself short.'

Out of the Rat-race and off on Your Own

If you don't like the idea of plunging straight into your executive suit the day after graduation, you may find the idea of voluntary work and travelling an appealing prospect before you settle down to the mundanity of a grown-up existence. More and more graduates are pursuing the option of working abroad and engaging in a little 'self-exploration' before they join the rat-race, and future rat-race employers look very favourably on those who have taken time out to travel, to work abroad or to do voluntary work. Again, a visit to your college careers office should enlighten you about some of the opportunities available and the organizations which operate in finding placements for graduates, whether it's teaching in Japan or building wells in Africa. Do as much research as soon as you can. It helps to apply as early as possible as, like most graduate opportunities, they become more fiercely contested year on year.

Chapter 10 / **How to Handle the Job Hunt**

Finding a job is always hard work and is not for the faint of heart. You need vast reserves of resilience, persistence and determination. These days any advertised job tends to attract hundreds of applicants, so it could take some time (and a few rejections) before you finally strike it lucky.

First Steps

The best way to find out what a particular job is really like is to talk to people who do it, so call people in your target area and ask if they would be prepared to chat to you for fifteen to twenty minutes about their work. The worst they can do is say no – but you may be pleasantly surprised by the numbers of people who'll be happy to spare you some time. Choose your time well when you ring and take the person's job into account: a magazine editor, for example, will probably have a pile of proofs to read late in the afternoon; the producer of a live show won't want to hear from you minutes before the programme goes on air. Make it clear that you're just looking for information and are not expecting to be offered a job. As well as asking them what their work involves, you could sound them out about the state of the industry at the moment, trends in the way things are going or what employers look for. Don't abuse their generosity – if you asked for fifteen minutes of their time, try not to take up more, unless they're obviously happy to carry on – and remember to send a thank-you letter soon after.

If your research reveals obvious gaps in your training or knowledge, do something about it, whether it's enrolling on a word-processing course or attending an industry conference. As well as improving your skills base, you'll also be providing an employer with a positive demonstration of your commitment and enthusiasm.

Make sure you *know* about the industry. Read the specialist press and relevant pages of the newspapers so that you're up to date on the issues affecting it. That way, you'll also know when companies are expanding or have won new contracts and might therefore be looking to recruit more staff.

While you're still at university you need to start gathering skills, practical experience and training as soon as possible to give you the edge over all the other thousands of graduates who'll be chasing jobs and postgraduate courses in the same field. Make the most of any free training on offer, in computing or languages, for example, which can be useful skills in many jobs.

The one thing that will count for more than most is relevant work experience and as much of it as possible, so good vacation jobs are vital. If you have secretarial skills, you may be able to find temping work. The other way of getting that all-important experience (and real insider view) is by offering to work for free. A good work placement will teach you more about the job than any careers book or counsellor can and the experience gained can be more valuable than all the paper qualifications in the world when it comes to getting a permanent job. It's also a chance to make useful contacts and, if it goes well, will stand you in good stead when vacancies come up. *Cosmopolitan* has filled several junior positions by employing people who made a good impression on work experience. You're unlikely to be paid but some companies will cover your expenses – look on it as an investment.

Making the Most of Work Experience

- Lots of students look for work experience in the holidays, so you're more likely to get in if you can work during term-time. Apply at least a couple of months in advance, as it can be difficult to get a place.

- When you apply, state exactly what area of work you're interested in and enclose a full CV. Give evidence of your interest, say what you hope to achieve and what they'll gain from having you.
- Be reliable. Even though you're not getting paid a fortune (if at all) you should behave professionally, arriving on time and not leaving before the end of the working day.
- Most of the work you're given will be thoroughly mundane (would *you* trust an inexperienced student with anything else?) but if you do the photocopying and tea-making with good grace you'll make a good impression. Do it with enthusiasm (or even offer before asked) and you'll definitely be remembered. However boring the tasks, do them all *well*: every little detail matters.
- It's always better to ask questions if you're doing something you don't understand than to blunder ahead and get it wrong. But whenever you ask a question, pay attention to the answer and write everything down so you don't irritate people by asking the same things over and over again.
- Remember people's names: draw a plan of the office with names by desks to jog your memory.
- Try to move around departments to get a flavour of each, rather than staying on one desk the whole time.
- How you handle people on the phone will be noticed, so be polite, try to sound authoritative and make sure when you take messages that you get the person's name and number and note down the date and time. Watch how other people deal with callers for hints on how to behave. Don't take the opportunity of the 'free' phones to call all your friends – if you must make a personal call, ask permission first.
- Use your initiative. If someone looks really busy, offer to help; if the phone rings at an empty desk, answer it. Ask if there's any outstanding filing you could do or if the bookshelves need tidying. If there's really nothing, use the time to practise on the computer.
- If the placement was successful, ask someone you worked closely with if they would provide a reference for you. Try to get them to do it before you leave or very soon after, before they forget

who you are. If there's anyone you get on particularly well with, stay in contact and let them know you'd love to hear when any jobs are going.

Finding a Job

When you see a job ad that interests you, study it carefully. What sort of qualities and experience do you think the interviewer is looking for? How can you demonstrate that you have them? Don't be afraid to apply for a job just because you don't have every single quality asked for in the ad – employers know that there is rarely such a creature as the totally perfect candidate. As long as you meet *most* of the requirements, you're in with a chance.

However, sitting back and waiting for the perfect ad to appear in the paper could take years – so don't. Go out looking instead. It's been estimated that only ten per cent of people find jobs by answering newspaper ads and many employers try to cut costs and avoid a deluge of applications by relying on word of mouth to find suitable candidates.

Write directly to the person in charge of the department, rather than to personnel, and specify the kind of work you're looking for. Your letter may then be passed on to personnel but not before it's been seen by the person who really makes the decisions about who to employ.

Networking is one of the best ways of finding a job so increase your visibility and experience by attending relevant courses or industry conferences, talks, etcetera. If anyone you know is employed in a company you want to work for, ask them to keep an ear to the ground and an eye on the in-house notice-boards and magazines to find out if any jobs are going. Some companies offer a cash incentive to employers who can introduce new staff to the company and save them advertising the job.

The Perfect CV

The purpose of a CV is to get you an interview – and that applies whether you're writing to an employer on spec or applying for an advertised vacancy. The idea is to make it a tempting taster so that they'll want to find out more. It's not meant to tell the whole story of your life and should never be more than two sides long – no employer is going to want to read more than that. For recent graduates, one page is enough. Tailor your CV to each different job you apply for, emphasizing or downplaying different aspects as relevant. The fact that you spent several vacations working in catering may be of limited interest if you're applying for a job at a women's glossy magazine – but if you're being interviewed by a hotel and catering trade publication, it could provide relevant experience and knowledge of the industry. Remember to adapt your CV as the years go on, adding, cutting and rewriting. For example, the further away you get from your schooldays, the less relevant your GCSEs become, so prune back the details as more relevant experience supersedes them. Nor do you need to carry on putting down the holiday job you did when you were sixteen.

There are many different styles of CV and it's largely a question of taste which you choose. The traditional and most widely recognized CV is one that follows a chronological format. After your basic personal details (name, address, telephone number, date of birth, nationality), give your career history, starting with your current or most recent job first, and working backwards. State the job title, company name, period of employment, brief job description and any special achievements. Describe your current job in most detail; be more succinct about ones before that. After Career History, list Educational Qualifications, again working backwards. You may also wish to include Other Information (for example, driving licence, foreign languages, computer skills).

Another option is a targeted CV, best used when you're applying for jobs on spec rather than in response to specific job advertisements. The emphasis is on aiming for a specific position and explaining why you're qualified for it. Under the heading 'Job Target' state the position you're aiming for, then, under headings such as 'Capabilities' and 'Achievements', list your skills and talents which relate to your prospective position and what you've done so far that shows you'd be able to perform in the job. Further headings should include 'Work Experience' and 'Education', as on a chronological CV.

Whichever format you choose, there are certain basic rules to follow:

- Use good quality white or off-white paper. Avoid anything fancy or gimmicky.
- Make the layout as attractive and accessible as possible: use a clear, easy-to-read typeface and leave wide margins and spaces between sections.
- Avoid long sentences. An employer wants to see the key facts at a glance and won't be impressed by rambling prose. Keep phrases short, punchy and active, starting with a verb, for example, 'developed new programme strand', 'improved copy flow system'. You don't need to say 'I' every time – who else would you be talking about in your CV?
- Cut out anything that's not essential. You don't need to include addresses of employers or educational institutions. If you have a degree it's not necessary to itemize every GCSE subject and grade.
- A CV should always be typed – and *well* typed. If you can't do it yourself or don't have access to a machine, get someone who can and does to do it for you.
- There's no need to include referees here unless you have such stunningly good ones that it would impress an employer. Never give anyone's name as a referee without checking with them first.
- Check, double check and triple check your CV – then give it to a friend to check again. Any mistakes will count against you.
- Eliminate the negative. A CV is a selling document, not the place to advertise every exam you've ever failed or career setback you've faced.

- Include interests and hobbies if you have little work experience as yet; otherwise, leave them off unless they demonstrate a skill or quality relevant to the job or are so unusual that they will intrigue the interviewer.
- If applying for jobs abroad, enclose a passport photograph of yourself – it's far more common to do this in other European countries than it is here.
- If you're responding to a job advertisement, make sure that the skills you highlight in your CV match those specified in the ad.
- Extra skills such as computer literacy and foreign languages are valuable, but don't make them up to impress. If you claim to have fluent French, for example, you could find an interviewer asking you some questions in that language.

Positive/active words that stand out on CVs

achieved • administered • analysed • built • capable
communicated • competent • consistent • controlled
coordinated • created • designed • developed • directed
economical • edited • effective • efficient • established
expanded • experienced • guided • implemented • improved
increased • initiated • introduced • led • managed • monitored
organized • participated • positive • processed • produced
professional • proficient • profitable • qualified • repaired
researched • resourceful • responsible • skilled • sold
specialized • stable • successful • supervised • trained
versatile • volunteered • wrote

The Covering Letter

Never send off a CV or application form without a covering letter – it's missing a great opportunity to sell yourself. (If you have a glowing testimonial or letter of recommendation from a former employer, you could enclose that too.) Keep it short and to the point: it should fit on to one sheet, preferably on the same, high quality, paper as your CV.

Put your address in the top right-hand corner or centred at the top of the page, and the date and address of the person you're sending it to below that on the left-hand side. Make sure you address the letter to someone by name rather than 'the Personnel Officer' or 'Dear Sir/Madam'. Call the company first to find out, and always check the spelling. The correct ending to a letter addressed to a person by name is 'Yours sincerely' ('Yours faithfully' is used only when the addressee is Dear Sir or Dear Madam).

Make sure the letter is tidy – if there are lots of applicants for a job, it's easy to start by discarding the ones whose replies are scruffy or ill-prepared. Typing looks smarter, unless the employer specifically requests a handwritten letter, in which case draft it on a rough piece of paper first, so that you can write the final letter without mistakes. Use blue or (preferably) black ink; other colours are generally frowned upon and green ink is considered the trademark of a loony.

With any job application, it's important that your spelling, grammar and punctuation should be correct.

If you're applying for a specific job, say how you heard about it and if there is a reference number, include it. If you're writing at the suggestion of someone the employer knows personally or someone who is well known in the field, then mention it straight away. Keep the language simple: many people make the mistake of using over-formal, flowery phrases which just sound stilted and unnatural. State briefly why you are a strong candidate and emphasize what you have to offer the employer: 'As music editor of the university newspaper, I have had plenty of experience in dealing with PRs and celebrities, interviewing and writing, and have acquired a number of valuable contacts.' It is not good enough to say 'I'd love to work for your company'. So would a million others. Draw attention to the relevant bits of your CV but don't go into details – save that for the interview.

Don't write a fabulous letter, then ruin the effect by cramming it into a tiny little envelope. Your paper should never be folded more than twice, so make sure your envelope is A4, A5 or 220 × 110 mm-size.

Application Forms

Many companies, especially large organizations, ask all job applicants to fill in an application form, rather than sending in a CV. It makes it easier for them to find the information they need to know quickly, which is invaluable when dealing with large numbers of applicants.

Photocopy the blank form and do a rough version of your answers on the photocopy first, then once you're happy with it, copy them on to the original. Complete all sections, however irrelevant they might seem. Don't leave the Further Information box blank – it's missing a chance to shine and say things you haven't had the opportunity to say elsewhere. Look back at the job ad to see what they were asking for and if you haven't had a chance to prove how well you match the description anywhere else, now's your chance. Write legibly and in black ink: the form will probably be photocopied and blue ink doesn't photocopy well.

Take a photocopy of the finished form as a useful reference for the next time you have to fill one in.

Interviews

Interviews can be nerve-racking, especially for first-time job-hunters – and the more you want the job, the worse it is. Nerves come, in a large part, from feeling unready and unprepared, so the more you plan ahead, the better your chances and the better you'll feel on the day. Research may be time-consuming but it's worth it: it shows initiative and motivation and will give you a great advantage over candidates who haven't bothered. If you're ignorant about the company's work, then you're obviously not that interested in them or, presumably, the job. Don't be careless – confusing the company's products with those of a rival won't win you any friends.

Whatever the job you're going for, the following tips apply.

- Expect to be asked about your personal life and leisure interests as well as strictly work issues. The employer is trying to put together a picture of you as a complete person.
- If you've done some work already, prepare a clear, succinct précis of it and be prepared to answer questions on any aspect of it. Past performance is the main thing employers have to rely on when it comes to assessing how well you would do with them – so make sure you feed them relevant examples of past experience. How have you shown initiative, reliability, creativity, organizational flair, etcetera? Can you work well under pressure or adapt to changing conditions? What computer systems can you use?
- Be ready to explain why you're interested in this job. Sounds obvious, yes, but it's surprising how many people don't think it through.
- Straightforward questions about your studies, qualifications or job history are relatively easy to answer and you should certainly expect to be asked any of the questions in the box. Many interviews are relatively informal chats but there are always some interviewers who like to spring horrors such as 'How would your best friend/worst enemy/colleagues describe you?' or 'What are your strengths/weaknesses?' on you. You're unlikely to think of something suitable on the spot so it helps to think ahead and have examples prepared. *Great Answers to Tough Interview Questions* by Martin John Yate (Kogan Page, £6.99) has some great tips on how to avoid potential clangers.
- If you're going for your first job after university, you're unlikely to have much work experience, so you'll have to look to other areas for skills and experience to offer employers. Did you participate in team sports? Write for the school magazine? Make short films with the film society? Take leading roles in school plays? Serve on a hall of residence committee? Deliver seminars?

Questions you're likely to be asked

Tell me about yourself.
What makes you right for this job?
Why do you want to work for us?
Where do you see yourself in five years' time?
What computer systems have you worked on?
How do you feel about working long hours?

Undertake extensive or unusual travel during vacations? Have you done voluntary work, served time on a local community committee or been involved in an advisory board? Done any work placements during the holidays? Be prepared to answer questions about why you did these things and what you feel you've gained from them. Even things that seem irrelevant to you may help give an employer a fuller picture of you.

- As much as anything, they want evidence that you are reliable and responsible so even irrelevant work experience at weekends or in vacations could illustrate those qualities. If you've paid for any postgraduate studies yourself, it shows strong motivation and commitment so make sure you mention it.

- If you're a bit rusty at interviews try to run the whole thing through with a more practised friend beforehand, getting her to play the interviewer – she may come up with more possible questions you hadn't thought of. You may feel silly at first but it *will* help. Ask for honest feedback and don't get upset or defensive if there are negative points, as that will just discourage further comment. Don't over-rehearse or you'll end up sounding stilted and unnatural when you want to appear spontaneous and relaxed.

- You don't always get much notice of an interview so don't leave all your preparation until the letter arrives – start thinking about it when you make your application.

- Don't spend so long worrying about the questions you'll be asked that you forget the basics. Get plenty of sleep the night before the interview. Work out in advance how you're going to get there and how long it will take – and allow extra time for delays. Make sure a couple of days ahead that your clothes are clean and ready.

On the Day

Getting in the Mood

- Be positive! If you've been asked for an interview, they're obviously interested in you. To get to this stage you've probably already beaten hundreds of others and may be on a short list of between six and twelve. The employer already believes you are *capable* of the job – all you have to do is prove it.
- Do anything to help boost your confidence: read a favourite poem or inspirational book on the way to the interview, listen to 'up' music on your Walkman, remind yourself of all the times you've triumphed against the odds or all the things you've done that make you feel proud.
- Reread your letter/CV/application form and be ready to answer questions on anything you've included. Take copies with you in case the interviewer has mislaid them.
- Take a spare pair of tights, needle and cotton (for emergency repairs), Phonecard and small change (for parking or phone calls). Make sure you have the company's phone number so you can call in an emergency. And don't forget to take their address.
- Set out in plenty of time and aim to arrive ten to fifteen minutes early. Don't expect buses or trains to turn up on time or assume that you'll find a parking space easily. Use your waiting time to watch the people around you, read any internal notice-boards or in-house newsletters, and generally try to get a feel for the place.
- Don't smoke or drink shortly before the interview – smelling of smoke or alcohol isn't going to impress any interviewer.

Looking the Part

Don't underestimate the importance of appearance. Research has shown that an interviewer's impression of you will be made up of fifty-five percent how you look, thirty-eight per cent on how you sound and only seven per cent on the actual content of what you say. First impressions are quickly formed and hard to change and though your interview might last an hour, a decision has probably been largely made within the first four or five minutes.

- Your clothes don't need to be expensive – nobody expects someone fresh out of college to waltz in in Armani – but they must be presentable and clean. Make sure they're comfortable, too: you can't concentrate on the interview if you're too busy worrying about wayward buttons or squirming around because your skirt's too tight.
- Heels look smarter than flat – but not *too* high – and studies suggest that wearing light, natural make-up rather than none at all increases your chances of success by twenty per cent.
- Don't smoke, even if invited to do so – it looks messy. And unless you're ultra-relaxed refuse any offers of tea or coffee as well – they just provide more scope for disaster.
- Dress appropriately for the organization. As a general rule, think smart rather than trendy. Some experts recommend going to watch staff leaving or entering the workplace, so you can get an idea of the corporate image and tailor your interview outfit accordingly (same kind of clothes but a bit smarter).
- Don't go in to the interview room clutching carrier bags of shopping or a dripping wet coat and umbrella; leave any encumbrances with the receptionist to look after.
- Try and appear confident, even if you're quaking inside. Walk in confidently and sit upright but relaxed in the chair. Leaning slightly forward shows attention and interest. Look the interviewer in the eye but don't fix her with an unwavering stare. Speak up and, if you tend to gabble when nervous, make a conscious effort

to speak more slowly. Try to sound enthusiastic. Keep your arms and legs uncrossed, don't shift around in your seat and try not to fiddle with jewellery or your hair. Merely sitting comfortably gives you the desired impression of calm and confidence.

- However nervous you feel, *smile*! Most interviewers base their final decisions on gut feeling, and it's only natural that they will warm more to someone who appears relaxed and friendly, someone they think will be pleasant to work with as well as able to do the job.
- Don't save your best behaviour for the interviewer alone: be just as pleasant to the receptionist and anyone else you make contact with – they may be asked for their impressions.

In the Interview

- If the interviewer starts by asking you a few general questions like how your journey to the interview was, they're only trying to put you at your ease – don't go into great detail.
- A bit of humour or wit at appropriate moments will make you more memorable to an interviewer and provide a bit of light relief in what is, for her, probably a rather dull day of grilling nervous candidates.
- Concentrate on listening properly to what the interviewer is saying, rather than fretting about how you're doing and what she might ask next. If you miss something or are confused by a question, it's better to ask for clarification than to waffle on with an inappropriate answer. Keep your answers relevant.
- It's normal to play up your good points and try to skim over the bad ones. But you don't want to look as if you have something to hide, so if the interviewer does ask about any area you'd hoped to avoid (a previous redundancy, say, or a series of short-term jobs) answer briefly but honestly.
- Be specific in your answers. If you're asked how you would handle situation x, for example, say how you dealt successfully with a similar situation in the past.

- Employers do usually take up references so don't lie about something a referee might be asked to corroborate.
- Panel or board interviews can be especially daunting but at least you're less at the whim of one person's likes and dislikes. Sit somewhere where you can see everyone and they can all see you – if the chair's in the wrong place, move it. Members of the panel usually take it in turns to ask questions and you should watch the questioner as she talks to you, then address your answers mainly to her, but include the other panel members with occasional eye contact. Return your gaze to the chairperson at the end. If possible, find out in advance who the members of the panel will be. Try to memorize the names and to be equally polite and friendly to all members whatever their manner. When you get your turn to answer questions, direct them to the chair – she can then redirect them to the appropriate member of the panel.
- If there's a silence after you've given your answer to a question, don't feel you have to blunder in and fill it. Just ask the interviewer if you've made yourself clear and put the ball firmly back in their court.
- If you're asked about your hobbies and interests, don't say anything you can't back up. If you say you're keen on the theatre, for example, expect to be asked what is the best play you've seen recently.
- Remember, this is a two-way process: it's a time for you to find out about the potential employer and the job as well as vice versa, so don't miss your chance when asked if you have any questions. It also provides another opportunity for you to impress. Prepare three or four intelligent questions that demonstrate your genuine interest in the job or your familiarity with the business and the challenges facing it. Write them down on an index card if you think you might forget them and keep it conveniently to hand. If the interviewer doesn't offer you the chance to ask questions, then volunteer, but remember that asking too many is as bad as asking none at all. Be sensitive about time and alert to signs of impatience in the interviewer – remember, the next candidate is probably

waiting. If all your questions have been answered during the course of the interview, then say so.

- Questions about childcare and marital status are illegal but that doesn't stop some people asking them. If you want the job, it's probably best just to deal with them briefly but assure them that you can cope and wouldn't have applied for the job otherwise.
- Don't leave the interview without asking how soon you can expect to hear from them.

Money Matters

Many people will just accept whatever money is offered in their relief at getting the job, but salary is almost always open to negotiation, providing you go about it in the right way.

Before you go to an interview, try to find out what the going rate for the job is. Ask people working in the industry; contact professional associations; look at similar job ads to see if they mention money.

If the employer is unmovable on the money or won't go as high as you'd like, think about other areas that might be open to negotiation, such as flexible working hours, an early salary appraisal, training opportunities, a company car.

After the Interview

Assess your performance and see if there's anything you can learn from it. What went well? What went badly? If there were any questions that caught you out, brush up your answers for next time. If, despite all your best efforts, the interview was a disaster, don't automatically blame yourself. If you're unlucky enough to land an unpleasant or aggressive interviewer, you'll just have to write it off to experience and remind yourself that the next one can only be better. Review it in your mind to see if you can learn from it – then forget it and prepare for the next one.

However the interview went, it's a good idea to write the next day, thanking the interviewer for seeing you, reinforcing any important points and adding any extra relevant information you might have forgotten or been unable to pass on at the time. Keep it short and sweet – just enough to nudge the interviewer's memory and show that you really are keen. If you don't hear anything within the time expected, write or call to find out the state of play. Let them know if you have other interviews/offers to consider but don't make it sound like a threat. After the initial enquiry, leave it – hassling only irritates people.

If you're offered the job, clarify all terms and conditions before accepting. If you wait until you're in the job before sorting things out, you're in a weaker position to bargain. Don't hand in your notice in your current job until you have something in writing from your new employer – a verbal offer can be withdrawn.

If you don't get the job but you're still keen to work for the company, write and say you were sorry to be unsuccessful this time but would like to be kept on file in case of future vacancies. It wouldn't hurt to ask what the person who was appointed had that you didn't. Make it clear you're just looking for helpful feedback, not demanding explanations. At least it might give you something useful to take away from the experience rather than seeing it as a total failure.

Keeping up morale is important. It can be discouraging when you apply unsuccessfully for a string of jobs, especially when your friends are all finding their dream jobs, but don't let yourself sink into depression. Treat each interview as practice and remember that if you take great care over your letters and CVs you're already streets ahead of most people. Your time will come.

Chapter 11 / **Further Information**

Helpful Numbers

All the numbers listed are for the UK. Check your telephone directory or call the numbers below if you want to contact the local branch of these organizations.

Money and Debt

National Debtline
Telephone: 0121 359 8501
Offers advice, information and support on all sorts of financial problems, from debt to harassment by creditors to problems with banks.

Credit Action Freephone Helpline
Telephone: 0800 591 084
A helpline service specifically for students with financial problems, providing support, advice and counselling on debt and financial crises.

Grants and Loans

Student Loan Company
Telephone: 0800 405010
For advice and information on obtaining a student loan and on repayments, deferment and default on loans.

Department for Education and Employment
Sanctuary Buildings,
Great Smith Street,
London SW1P 3BT
Telephone: 0171 925 5000
Provides information on grants and loans for students in England and Wales.

Scottish Office Education Department
Gyle View House,
3 Redheughs Rigg, South Gyle,
Edinburgh EH12 9HH
Telephone: 0131 244 5823
Information and advice for students in Scotland.

Department of Education for Northern Ireland
Rathgael House, Balloo Road,
Bangor, Co Down BT19 7PR
Telephone: 01247 279279
Advice and information for students in Northern Ireland.

Education Grants Advisory Service (EGAS)
c/o Family Welfare Association,
501–502 Kingsland Road,
Dalston, London E8 4AU
Telephone: 0171 254 6251
Part of the Family Welfare Association, providing help, information and advice to students on grants and money to study.

Career Development Loans
Telephone: 0800 585 505
Freephone for free booklet on career development loans, which can cover costs such as course fees and other course costs if you can't get a grant.

Department of Social Security Freephone
Telephone: 0800 666555
Advice on social security benefits, including child support, housing benefits and income support.

Your Rights

NUS UK
Nelson Mandela House,
461 Holloway Road,
London N7 6LJ
E-mail: nus@nus.org.uk
Telephone: 0171 272 8900
NUS can provide students and student unions with advice, support and information on all sorts of issues, from legal problems, housing, health, education rights, exam appeals, student discounts, grants, loans and benefits right through to hiring bands or setting up student newspapers. They can also put you in touch with support groups for lesbian, gay and bisexual students, women student groups, mature students, students with disabilities and many other student groups on a local and national level.

There are also offices in Scotland, Wales and Northern Ireland.

NUS Scotland
11 Broughton Market,
Edinburgh EH3 6NU
Telephone: 0131 556 6598

NUS Wales/UCMC
107 Walter Road,
Swansea SA1 5QQ
Telephone: 01792 643323

NUS/Union of Students in Ireland
29 Bedford Street,
Belfast BT2 7EJ
Telephone: 01232 244641

Racism and Racial Equality

Commission for Racial Equality
Telephone: 0171 828 7022
Advice on issues of racism, racial prejudice and equal opportunities. Can provide legal advice and support.

Campus Watch
Telephone: 01426 942826
National twenty-four-hour phone line set up by NUS and the anti-fascism group Searchlight, for students to report incidents of racism on campus, including assaults, leafleting and graffiti.

Lesbian, Gay and Bisexual Students' Rights

Stonewall
Telephone: 0171 336 8860
Offers advice and support for lesbian, gay and bisexual people on a range of issues, including legal problems and equal rights. They can also put you in touch with local support groups.

Students with Disabilities' Rights

Disability Alliance
Telephone: 0171-247 8776
Offers advice and support for students with disabilities.

SKILL
Telephone: 0171 274 0565
Support and advice for students with disabilities.

International Students' Rights

UKCOSA
Telephone: 0171 226 3762
For overseas and international students studying within the United Kingdom, can offer legal advice and support on a range of issues including immigration, finance and education rights.

Housing Rights

Campaign for Bedsit Rights
Telephone: 0171 377 0027
Advice on all sorts of housing matters for people renting property, including legal rights, health and safety, and fair rents.

Shelter
Telephone: 0171 253 0202
National campaigning organization on homelessness. They can also put you in touch with their network of regional housing advice centres and they produce a range of publications on housing issues.

Safety and Crime

Victim Support
Telephone: 0171 735 9166
Emotional and practical advice for victims of crime. They can refer you to local support groups.

AA Emergency Breakdown
Telephone: 0800 66 77 88
For emergency help with car breakdowns and accidents.
Non-members can join on the spot.

Rape Crisis Centre
P.O. Box 69,
London WC1X 5NJ
Telephone: 0171 837 1600
Offers counselling and advice to women who have been raped or sexually assaulted at any time in their lives.

Endsleigh Insurance
Telephone: 01242 574242 (Head office)
The insurance company set up originally by NUS to provide insurance designed to meet the needs of students. Contact the head office for details of the branch nearest to you.

Credit Card Loss

Access, NatWest: 0113 277 8899
Access, Lloyds: 0800 585300
American Express: 01273 696933
Barclaycard/Visa: 01604 230230
Co-operative Bank/Visa: 01695 26621
Mastercard/Eurocard: 01702 362988
Bank of Scotland/Visa: 01383 738866

Drink, Drugs and Smoking

Alcoholics Anonymous
Telephone: 01904 644026
Advice and support for people suffering from alcoholism or with a drink problem.

Drinkline
Telephone: 0345 320202
National helpline with advice on sensible limits for drinking and advice on cutting down on alcohol.

National Drugs Helpline
Telephone: 0800 77 66 00
Twenty-four-hour freephone national helpline on all issues relating to drug use, and advice and counselling for family, friends and carers or drug users.

Quitline
Telephone: 0800 00 22 00
Freephone helpline for smokers who want to quit and for ex-smokers, partners, friends and families.

AIDS and HIV

National AIDS Helpline
Telephone: 0800 567123
Advice and support on all issues of safer sex, HIV and AIDS.

Terence Higgins Trust Helpline
Telephone: 0171 242 1010
Advice and support on all issues of safer sex, HIV and AIDS.

Depression, Loneliness and Mental Illness

British Association for Counselling
Telephone: 01788 578323
Can provide details of local counselling services.

Saneline
2nd Floor,
199–205 Old Marylebone Road,
London NW2 5QP

Telephone: 0345 678000
Offers advice and support for people coping with mental illness, crisis support and information.

Samaritans
Telephone: 0345 90 90 90
For help, support and advice for anyone needing emotional support or experiencing suicidal feelings.

Women's Health

Healthline
Telephone: 0345 678444
National helpline covering a wide variety of health issues.

National Association for Pre-Menstrual Syndrome
Telephone: 01732 741709
National helpline for women suffering from PMS, offering listening and information, including advice on diet and medical treatments.

Women's Nationwide Cancer Control Campaign
Telephone: 0171 729 2229
National helpline for women and their friends and families on all issues relating to cancer and cancer screening, particularly breast and cervical cancers. They can also send information and refer you to local advice centres.

Women's Health
Telephone: 0171 251 6580
Helpline for advice on all issues of women's health, including gynaecological problems.

Eating Disorders

Anorexia and Bulimia Anonymous
Telephone: 0181 748 3994
Twenty-four-hour counselling, support and advice for people suffering from eating disorders.

Eating Disorders Association
Telephone: 01603 621414
National helpline for sufferers of eating disorders and for their families and friends. They can also put you in touch with a network of support groups throughout the United Kingdom.

Pregnancy, Contraception and Abortion

Brook Advisory Centres
Telephone: 0171 323 1522
For advice on contraception, pregnancy, abortion and sexual problems.

Family Planning Association
Telephone: 0171 636 7866
Run by the National Health Service, a vast network of Family Planning Clinics offers advice on contraception, sexual health, pregnancy and abortion.

Pregnancy Advisory Service
Telephone: 0171 637 8962
Provides advice and counselling on pregnancy and abortion.

READ MORE IN PENGUIN

BUSINESS AND ECONOMICS

In with the Euro, Out with the Pound   Christopher Johnson

The European Union is committed to setting up the Euro as a single currency, yet Britain has held back, with both politicians and public unable to make up their minds. In this timely, convincing analysis, Christopher Johnson asserts that this 'wait and see' policy is damaging and will result in far less favourable entry terms.

Lloyds Bank Tax Guide   Sara Williams and John Willman

An average employee tax bill is over £4,000 a year. But how much time do you spend checking it? Four out of ten never check the bill – and most spend less than an hour. Mistakes happen. This guide can save YOU money. 'An unstuffy read, packed with sound information' – *Observer*

The Penguin Companion to European Union
Timothy Bainbridge with Anthony Teasdale

A balanced, comprehensive picture of the institutions, personalities, arguments and political pressures that have shaped Europe since the end of the Second World War.

Understanding Offices   Joanna Eley and Alexi F. Marmot

Few companies systematically treat space as a scarce resource or make conscious efforts to get the best from their buildings. This book offers guidance on image, safety, comfort, amenities, energy-efficiency, value for money and much more.

Faith and Credit   Susan George and Fabrizio Sabelli

In its fifty years of existence, the World Bank has influenced more lives in the Third World than any other institution, yet remains largely unknown, even enigmatic. This richly illuminating and lively overview examines the policies of the Bank, its internal culture and the interests it serves.

READ MORE IN PENGUIN

HISTORY

Citizens Simon Schama

The award-winning chronicle of the French Revolution. 'The most marvellous book I have read about the French Revolution in the last fifty years' – Richard Cobb in *The Times*

The Lure of the Sea Alain Corbin

Alain Corbin's wonderful book explores the dramatic change in Western attitude towards the sea and seaside pleasures that occured between 1750 and 1840. 'A compact and brilliant taxonomy of the shifting meanings of the sea and shore' – *New York Review of Books*

The Tyranny of History W. J. F. Jenner

A fifth of the world's population lives within the boundaries of China, a vast empire barely under the control of the repressive ruling Communist regime. Beneath the economic boom China is in a state of crisis that goes far deeper than the problems of its current leaders to a value system that is rooted in the autocratic traditions of China's past.

The English Bible and the Seventeenth-Century Revolution
Christopher Hill

'What caused the English civil war? What brought Charles I to the scaffold?' Answer to both questions: the Bible. To sustain this provocative thesis, Christopher Hill's new book maps English intellectual history from the Reformation to 1660, showing how scripture dominated every department of thought from sexual relations to political theory ... 'His erudition is staggering' – *Sunday Times*

Fisher's Face Jan Morris

'*Fisher's Face* is funny, touching and informed by wide reading as well as wide travelling' – *New Statesman & Society*. 'A richly beguiling picture of the Victorian Navy, its profound inner security, its glorious assumptions, its extravagant social life and its traditionally eccentric leaders' – *Independent on Sunday*

READ MORE IN PENGUIN

SCIENCE AND MATHEMATICS

About Time Paul Davies

'With his usual clarity and flair, Davies argues that time in the twentieth century is Einstein's time and sets out on a fascinating discussion of why Einstein's can't be the last word on the subject' – *Independent on Sunday*

Insanely Great Steven Levy

It was Apple's co-founder Steve Jobs who referred to the Mac as 'insanely great'. He was absolutely right: the machine that revolutionized the world of personal computing was and is great – yet the machinations behind its inception were nothing short of insane. 'A delightful and timely book' – *The New York Times Book Review*

Wonderful Life Stephen Jay Gould

'He weaves together three extraordinary themes – one palaeontological, one human, one theoretical and historical – as he discusses the discovery of the Burgess Shale, with its amazing, wonderfully preserved fossils – a time-capsule of the early Cambrian seas' – *Mail on Sunday*

The *New Scientist* Guide to Chaos Edited by Nina Hall

In this collection of incisive reports, acknowledged experts such as Ian Stewart, Robert May and Benoit Mandelbrot draw on the latest research to explain the roots of chaos in modern mathematics and physics.

Innumeracy John Allen Paulos

'An engaging compilation of anecdotes and observations about those circumstances in which a very simple piece of mathematical insight can save an awful lot of futility' – *The Times Educational Supplement*

Consciousness Explained Daniel C. Dennett

'Extraordinary ... Dennett outlines an alternative view of consciousness drawn partly from the world of computers and partly from the findings of neuroscience. Our brains, he argues, are more like parallel processors than the serial processors that lie at the heart of most computers in use today ... Supremely engaging and witty' – *Independent*

READ MORE IN PENGUIN

Cosmopolitan Career Guides: a series of lively and practical handbooks produced by *Cosmopolitan* writers on a wide range of subjects.

Cosmopolitan Guide to Working in Journalism and Publishing
Suzanne King

Careers in journalism and publishing are seen as highly desirable, but what exactly do they involve? Suzanne King describes the work undertaken by those in all sections of the industries, from newspaper reporter to magazine editor, TV researcher to radio PA, book commissioning editor to freelance writer. This expert guide also lists relevant training schemes and courses, salary ranges and numerous case histories, providing inspiration, insider information and invaluable advice.

Cosmopolitan Guide to Working in Retail
Elaine Robertson

The retailing business is the country's biggest employer, providing jobs for one in ten of the UK workforce. What kind of career oppurtunities can retail offer you? From window dresser to buyer, personal shopper to department manager, this informative book will help you choose the right career.

published or forthcoming:

Cosmopolitan Guide to Working in PR and Advertising
Robert Gray and Julia Hobsbawm
Cosmopolitan Guide to Getting Ahead in Your Career
Suzanne King
Cosmopolitan Guide to the Big Trip
Elaine Robertson and Suzanne King